The Modern Trombone

THE NEW INSTRUMENTATION

EDITORS
BERTRAM TURETZKY & BARNEY CHILDS

EXECUTIVE EDITOR
ALAIN HÉNON
UNIVERSITY OF CALIFORNIA PRESS

The Modern Trombone

A Definition of Its Idioms

STUART DEMPSTER

UNIVERSITY OF CALIFORNIA PRESS
Berkeley · Los Angeles · London

University of California Press
Berkeley and Los Angeles, California
University of California Press, Ltd.
London, England
© 1979 by
The Regents of the University of California
ISBN 0-520-03252-7
Library of Congress Catalog Card Number: 76-14309
Printed in the United States of America

1 2 3 4 5 6 7 8 9

To my wife,
Renko

Contents

Recorded Examples

The examples that will be found on the records that accompany this book are listed here by record side number. These examples are coordinated with the text, and in the margins of the text you will find the recorded example numbers adjacent to the relevant text discussion. In the list below, following each example, the text page number where the relevant text discussion occurs is given.

RECORDED EXAMPLES

Acknowledgments

Thanks go to so many it is impossible to know where to begin or end, but I will give it a try anyway. Thanks, then, to the following: Alain Hénon, University of California Press Editor, Barney Childs and Bertram Turetzky, *The New Instrumentation* Editors, for their assistance, reassurance, and patience; Jerrie Kennedy, who so kindly edited the entire manuscript; William Bergsma, Donald Erb, and Robert Erickson, for their suggestions after reading the first draft; Brad Sherman, for the hand-drawn examples; Mea Hartman, Al Swanson, and Betty Wangerin for their assistance in the preparation of the recordings; Buddy Baker, Glenn Bridges, John Cage, James Fulkerson, Frank Rehak, Bernard Schneider, Gerald Sloan, Larry Weed, and others, who wrote letters or otherwise supplied helpful information to me; Loren Rush and the Center for Computer Research in Music and Acoustics (CCRMA), Stanford University, for their assistance in the preparation of the index; the University of Washington for its direct and indirect support; the publishers who have given their permission to print musical examples, particularly Raoul Ronson of Seesaw-Okra Music Corp., who so willingly gave permission to reprint the entire *General Speech*; and finally the composers who have written the incredibly beautiful music that has made this book possible.

Foreword

This book is intended to extend the techniques discussed in other books rather than to supplant or compete with the books and methods now in existence. It will neither discuss nor ignore the traditional trombone, but will build upon that which already exists in trombone materials and orchestration books. Books to consult before reading this one would be the trombone books by Fink, Gregory, Kleinhammer, and Wick, as well as such basic orchestration books as those by Kennan and Piston. David Baker's *Contemporary Techniques for the Trombone* should also be examined with special attention to the value of exercises and drills. While Baker's book "addresses itself to the teacher, student, amateur and professional trombonist . . . ," this book is for *composers* as well as trombonists and, of course, teachers in both fields. Composers and trombonists alike need to be aware of those techniques that are idiomatic to the trombone.

Traditional technique cannot be ignored, since it is mandatory in order to learn and master new techniques; learning and mastering new techniques enhance and define more clearly traditional techniques. The old and the new, so seemingly separate, are actually inseparable and, in the long run, complementary, even if in the short run this seems not to be the case.

In examining the reasons why this condition exists, at least on a brass instrument and particularly on a trombone, I studied the Australian aboriginal didjeridu, a hollowed-out tree trunk that functions much like a trombone (see Appendix III). It turns out that much of what I thought was new is a two-thousand-year-old tradition! As far as can be determined, the aboriginals have been using many of these "new" sounds for centuries. This information led me to conclude that this treatise should be less concerned with what is *new* or *old* on the trombone than with what is *idiomatic* to the instrument. These idioms have been of foremost importance in my determination of the trombone's acoustical repertoire, which is the subject of the book.

The trombone is not an instrument in the usual sense, since it has no reed to make sound; rather, it is a *resonator* of whatever sound is introduced at the mouthpiece. This "non-instrument" is similar to a megaphone; its real function is to focus the sound rather than to amplify it. That is to say, the trombone primarily controls the quality of tone produced and, secondarily, increases the loudness. It is this quality of tone that produces the sound of a trombone rather than the sound of, say, a baritone horn. That the trombone can be simulated by a garden hose fitted with a mouthpiece and a funnel (for a bell) only clarifies the point that the garden hose is a nonadjustable-length trombone, just as the trombone is an adjustable-length garden hose.

The trombone is an extension of the self. The primary sound source, the buzzed lip, is located in, rather than at the end of, the resonating chamber; the body also functions as a resonator. The alteration of the mouth cavity, tongue, and throat, for instance, has a tremendous effect on the total trombone sound, and much if not more study time is generally spent on these aspects than on the actual buzzing itself. Thus, various chapters in this book, particularly the early ones, discuss body uses and possible alterations directly concerned with the production of tone or with quality change.

Each chapter is a unit and is designed to be read separately if desired. Chapters are cross-referenced in such a way that related topics from different chapters can be read consecutively. One can also read advantageously from back to front (see Backword). Once acquainted with the trombone's "palette of colors" through the reading of these chapters, one can begin to think about music that is truly idiomatic for the trombone.

This book is an invitation to experiment with the materials provided, and it is my fervent hope that the reader will do this frequently while reading the book. It is also an invitation for composers and performers to construct pieces together, and furthermore, to take the time necessary to become really acquainted with the trombone. While doing so, readers are encouraged to exercise the same diligence that is usually reserved for acquiring knowledge of the strings or piano. My own view — which may be a singular one — is that a composer and performer, when given the chance, can work together beneficially and produce works of a quality far greater than just the sum of the two people's efforts. Such collaborative works, all fully documented in the Bibliography, provide most of the examples for this book. My orientation is performance; that of the composers is, of course, composition; however, the best description of the collaboration, in Robert Erickson's own words, is the phrase, "Each gets into the other's pockets."

To mention Robert Erickson is to cite an individual who, perhaps, has thought about the trombone as a source of sound and sight more deeply than any other composer. This has been in part due to my own insistence, but, for whatever reason, he has devoted his sole attention to the trombone at least twice to produce two major works for trombone, the *Ricercare á 5* (1966) and *General Speech* (1969). Other equally important works are also collaborations, such as Luciano Berio's *Sequenza V* (1966) or Pauline Oliveros's *Theater Piece* (1966), the latter actually a three-way collaboration of Oliveros, choreographer Elizabeth Harris, and myself. Oliveros sees an instrument as assuming virtually the entire personality of the instrumentalist. No other person, so far as I know, works in quite this fashion. The point here is that none of these pieces could have attained their high artistic level without the aforementioned collaboration. I see true value in collaboration and find it preferable to composer and performer working separately in their separate towers (not necessarily ivory), rarely communicating. Granted, collaboration requires more work from each party, but each is then more satisfied and the long-term value is far more significant.

It has been my experience in the past to find many trombone players distraught at the sight of so many "difficult new pieces." Happily, this state of affairs is changing as trombonists begin to realize the tremendous acoustical potential of their instrument, and that they *can* exercise some control over their own artistic destiny. Indeed, trombonists should take responsibility in acquiring new literature, such as is being done through the International Trombone Association. The above organization, and the various trombone and brass workshops here and abroad, provide a convenient and comfortable structure from within which works can be commissioned. As good as the above-cited group effort is, however, individual endeavor will probably bring about even more fruitful results. If the individual trombonist can face this challenge by meeting composers and inspiring them to write *for him* or *her* as an instrument and, possibly, as a total personality, then my efforts will be more than amply rewarded.

Stuart Dempster
Seattle, Washington

Chapter I:
Voice and Multiphonics

A new study of the trombone is best begun with the most important secondary pitch source: the voice. Using the voice to produce harmony in the trombone dates at least to the turn of the century and possibly much earlier.[1] Probably the most famous early example in brass literature is in the C. M. von Weber *Horn Concertino*, Op. 45, during the cadenza.[2] While not a new idea, use of voice has appeared mostly in the back of method books as purely an exercise, and it seems likely that neither composer nor performer took much serious interest in it as a musical resource. During the second half of the present century, however, a tremendous interest has developed in this "double stop" technique to such a degree that it probably holds equal status with the vowel sounds as the most popular, successful, easily learned, and best organized of all the new techniques.

THE VOICE

Ia

If one is merely to speak into the trombone, the megaphone effect is easily observed. The best resonance is achieved by sealing the lips on the mouthpiece, just as one would naturally do for normal

Ib

playing. Speech is a good sound source, and although the distortion is significant, the words can still be understood.[3]

---

1. Glenn Bridges, in a letter dated 12 August 1974: "There were many who were good at it. Gardelle Simons was a master at this besides Pryor, Mantia, etc. I heard Mantia do the stunt on Euphonium back in the 1920s. Even old Innes did this when he came to this country in 1880. I would say it goes 'way back. I have little doubt but what it was done in England in the early 1800s. Many early cornet players did the stunt very early. In fact it is a well-known fact that ARBAN did all of these well-known stunts."

2. Larry Weed, in a letter dated 11 March 1975: "Birchard Coar's book on 19th-Century Horn Virtuosi credits Hampel with both stopped horn and simultaneous notes (circa 1786)."

3. In the Krenek *Five Pieces*, page 11, "muttering" is required. I like to think of things to say that are appropriate to the time, place, and audience; however, it should not be understood any more than muttering would be normally understood. It is followed in this particular case by a "bark," a dog bark that appears as well in other pieces such as in Cage's *Solo*. See the section on animal sounds in Chapter VI below.

To understand the voice alone, one can hum — with lips closed so the sound actually emanates from the nose — alternating with an open-lipped sound (a normal voice "ah"). I have termed this a "humsing," and the notation would be as in the following example:

Ic   Example 1: Humsing

It is not necessary to stick to "ma"; the sounds "mi" (mee), "mo" (moh), "mu" (moo), or "mi-a-o" (mee-ah-oh), etc. (cf. Chapter II) can also be used. Once again, the seal of the lips on the mouthpiece must be correct. The next step is to sing through the trombone just to get used to the idea. This is normally not interesting, though the sound is needed from time to time. The interest generally comes in its combination with the lip.

VOICE AND BUZZED LIP

After the voice alone, then, proceed with the unison (Example 2) and learn to keep this unison in tune and in even volume.

Id   Example 2: Unison

Then practice moving away from the unison, first by moving the slide a little down, then the voice a little down. Literally count the number of "beats" resulting from the intonation (these "beats" are requested in Donald Erb's . . . *and then, toward the end* . . . during the cadenza). Finally, reach the distance of a half step, stopping along the way to try and tune quarter tones. Practice all the intervals,

Ie   tune carefully, and listen to all the added tones or intonation beats. A major sixth or minor seventh, for instance, will give a three- or four-note result.

In producing double stops, most people prefer to keep the voice pitch above the lip pitch. The reverse seems harder to control even though it is used more than just occasionally, which will be seen later on. Perhaps the most important thing to keep in mind is that one must "shout" the voice through the instrument while at the same time allowing a "breathy" lip sound to go through. This is because both sounds (lip and voice) are functioning in the same chamber, and tricky balancing is necessary, therefore, to keep the two sounds relatively equal. The following example (3) is useful for mastering this balance.

If   Example 3: Unison with Alternating Dynamics

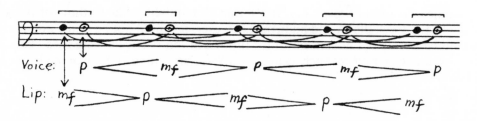

When this alternating dynamic exercise is practiced correctly, one will hear the same pitch with only a timbre change, which should be as slight as possible. Practice letting go and reattacking each timbre as it becomes soft, in such a way that the fade and return of a given timbre cannot be discerned.[4] Another practice technique and its variant are seen in Example 4.

Ig   Example 4: Glissed and Slurred Pitch Exchanges

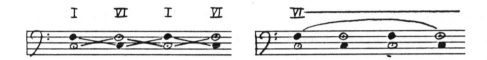

This is an exchange of the same two pitches from lip to voice to lip to voice, done by either glissando or just plain slurring. The slurred version can be practiced fast enough to be a trill effect and should be done occasionally. Keep in mind, however, that these techniques are in their elemental form and that it is quite possible to find them in more difficult parameters.

Ih   The next step would be to learn a chorale such as that which appears in Mueller's *Technical Studies*, Vol. II.[5] Mueller states that if the intonation is true, three- and four-note chords will sound. He further states that "such a chord certainly does not sound loud, but the player who can execute this trick well is sure to greatly surprise the listener."[6] The playing of chords is still a surprise to most people, but perhaps eventually it will be accepted as it properly should be — as another idiomatic sound. This is not a loud device, and the limit a composer should think of is mf, for if written any louder the voice cannot keep up.

The difficulty in mastering voice-lip double stops is akin to a piano student's first two-part piece in which the hands must act independently. The voice and lip must be able to go in different directions at the same time, but, when first learning this, the voice will want to vibrate sympathetically with the lip. After one overcomes this, the use of the voice-lip technique is easy and is one of the elementary steps of mastering the trombone.

Women will discover that many works have parts written too low for their voices, and the woman player must try octave displacement or other compromises in order to perform some of them. For instance, I occasionally find a piece that is out of my vocal range as well, but I have discovered that reversing the parts (the voice below the lip) will generally solve the problem. For these reasons, and because the voice used in conjunction with the lip loses a fair amount of the low range, composers are encouraged to write vocal parts that lie in a "second tenor" range (see Example 5).

---

4. It is not clear from Berio's notation, but this dynamic exchange is exactly the technique desired on the last note of his *Sequenza V*. At the very end, the bringing of the trombone down away from the lips while the vocal sound continues is marvelous as both an acoustical and a theatrical gesture.

5. Robert Mueller, *Technical Studies for Trombone* (New York: Carl Fischer, 1924), Vol. II, p. 58.

6. Ibid.

Example 5: Recommended Voice Range

Women may complain that this voice range is placed too low, but men may complain that it is too high! Nevertheless, the composer must have something to work with, and while men can, even if they often will not, scream a good fifth above the G indicated above, women can scream a good bit higher than that! The low range is of critical importance here because it is somewhat open-ended; however, most trombone players would be quite adamant about having any voice usage conform to the above example. Perhaps it would be best to compose "ossia" parts so that performers of either sex could use double stops the way the composer intended.

THE SCREAM

Ii   The voice in its high register (falsetto, for example) creates vast changes, and one can literally scream through the trombone to make loud sounds indeed. A study of the didjeridu (see Appendix III) shows that, like the voice in general, the scream is part of its performance tradition. The aboriginals use the high sound to imitate animals and the middle-range voice to produce chords. These sounds are not new, then, but are really idiomatic to the trombone (cf. Chapter VI).

Various vocal sounds, particularly the scream, can effectively mimic the sounds of electronic music.
Ij   A high scream, along with a low-played note, probably comes closest to a "ring modulator" effect. This sound can be coupled with vowels for an even more striking effect and is quite easy to do. To achieve more complexity, one can add a vowel mute, such as the wa-wa or plunger, thus allowing
Ik   two vowel changes simultaneously. The only danger here is that, because of the complexity, the effects cancel each other out; that is, when too many effects are performed at the same time, the texture becomes cluttered.

HIGH REGISTER CLOSE DOUBLE STOPPING

Il   One use of double stops that should be noted is the use of played-sung major and minor thirds in the high register. The special feature of these intervals is the production of low-register resultant or combination tones. It is unfortunate that these thirds must be played quite high to have the low tones brought up into the audible range, because high double stopping is fatiguing. It tires the throat and creates an unpleasant back pressure, so it is not advisable to continue for a long time.[7] One can also vary the low resultant tones by varying the interval up high, even moving into seconds or fourths.

---

7. Women, however, may find this a great deal easier than men, and there is, to my belief, a whole world of double stops, including these close intervals, available to women players that warrants extensive investigation.

When approaching seconds, however, the intonation "beats" emerge more prominently; in fourths, a more chord-like effect is achieved. In any case, the sound is so complex, it would not be advisable to use many — if any — other effects at the same time.

SPLIT TONE

Im   The split tone is another effect that clutters the texture. It is just what the name implies: a split — in this case, *between* two partials so that elements of both partials are heard.[8] This is a means of producing multiple sounds — a "multidivider" — not by using the voice, but by the lips breaking up into two embouchures. Theoretically this can be done between any two partials, but on the trombone the area between the second and third is best.[9] The procedure also may be used between the first and second and between the third and fourth partials, but both of these are unstable and should only be used with caution. The performer must hunt for the balance point between the two partials; this can be heard or, more properly perhaps, felt. One way to learn this technique is to lip slur back and fourth on the two partials, slowing down until the balance point is found. This slurring, by the way, is itself a useful device. Austin suggests that for this split tone effect one should "overblow,"[10] but this implies that the technique could not be done softly. Such is not the case, for it *can* be done softly rather well. Another useful idea is to glissando the split tone, which can, with practice, become very

In   smooth.

Mixing split tones with vocal double stops is possible but is usually not desirable, for the result lacks clarity and is too muddy and complex. The best mixing comes with the vowels or mutes, as noted earlier for the voice; however, it must be used with discretion.

BUZZED LIP AND MUTED VOWEL HARMONICS

Within the context of normal playing, certain vowel shapes can produce multiphonics.[11] The first step in producing a multiphonic effect is to play a long, low pitch, such as Bb in the bass clef staff.

----

8. There is another kind of split tone whereby the lip actually divides into octaves, two distinct pitches being heard. A few players can do this rather easily, whereas most seem to have quite a problem with it. I find myself in the latter category and suspect that it may be too unstable to be depended upon as a compositional device. A possible substitution is using the voice with the lip in octaves. Extended examples appear in Roger Reynolds's "*. . . From Behind the Unreasoning Mask" for Trombone, Percussion, and Tape*, recently released on New World Records NW 237.

9. Larry Austin, in his *CHANGES*, writes on page 6 and 7 only a fourth apart instead of a fifth apart for the second and third partials. It does not matter, really, since the effect is the same.

10. Ibid., page 6. James Fulkerson states that if one thinks of the pitch between the partials and tries to play that pitch it will be easier. Further, he also states that turning the lips out a little (like a pucker) will also help. I concur with Fulkerson, having tried his suggestions, and I find that these split tones are useful in a much wider range.

11. The method for producing the basic lip vowels that are necessary here are described in Chapter II under "Buzzed Vowels." Keep in mind that, in producing buzzed vowels, no voice is used. See also

Over this steady note one changes the vowels by changing the oral cavity. The idea is to do the change extremely slowly so that various partials of the Bb will be emphasized. It is possible, by stopping the change, to make any one of the partials prominent enough to be actually heard as a separate pitch. Since this pitch is heard in combination with the low drone note, a multiphonic is created.

These multiphonic effects are named "Vowel Harmonics," and as such are briefly mentioned under that heading in Chapter II. Example 6 below shows the playing range and the available partial spectrum.

Example 6: Playing Range and Oral Shaping Partial Spectrum Available

I consider the low Bb to F "best" range as the most "juicy" because when a player passes through the spectrum quickly (the vowel effect) a very liquid sound is produced. Passing through the spectrum slowly produces the multiphonic effect, as noted above. Wavering back and forth from two adjacent partials (the vibrato effect) is also very useful, and is discussed in Chapter V under "Tongue or Vowel Vibrato."

General Speech by Robert Erickson (see Appendix I) uses precisely the playing range shown in Example 6 with emphasis on the "best" or "juicy" pitches. It is not an accident (although I think it was probably unconscious) that the composer chose this range due to its speechlike quality and its resemblance to the male voice range. It is due to the use of these high partials that the piece becomes so intriguing. *General Speech* will be discussed in detail in Chapter II; in this discussion it is the settling down on one or another partial that is being examined.

If a Bb in the bass clef staff is played, the partials that can be emphasized are partials 8 through 12 (Bb, C, D, Eb, and F). If an F just below the bass clef staff is played, for instance, the choice in the spectrum is partials 11 through 16 (a sharp Bb, C, a sharp Db, a flat Eb, E, and F). Example 7 shows this graphically below:

Example 7: Multiphonic Choices on Low Bb and Low F

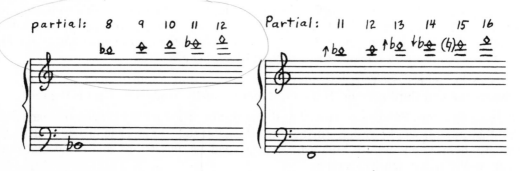

---

the section on the "Spectral Glide" in Robert Erickson's *Sound Structure in Music* (Los Angeles: University of California Press, 1975), pp. 72-75.

The wa-wa mute can also be used to produce a multiphonic effect. The hand opening and closing over the stem of the wa-wa is comparable to the vowels shaped by the oral cavity. An effective playing range is from Bb to F in the bass clef, and the partial spectrum available is from the D near the top of the treble clef staff to the C above (see Example 8). Notice how the behavior, although similar to the lip vowels, is in a much tighter overall range.

Example 8: Wa-wa Mute Ideal Playing Range and Partial Spectrum Available

Shown below, in Example 9, are the possibilities of two pitches within the range indicated in Example 8 above.

Iq

Ir

Example 9: Multiphonic Choices Using Wa-wa Mute on F and Bb

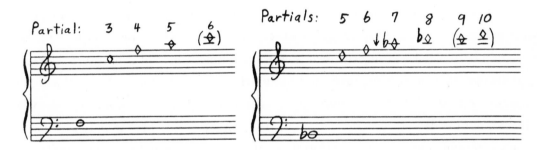

In both Examples 7 and 9, one should notice how, as one plays lower, the vowel spectrum is more densely populated; that is, one uses a higher set of partials even though the partials remain in the same pitch range. Contrast this with using the voice all by itself and altering the oral cavity, where the partials of the voice being altered, roughly partials 3 through 10, remain the same and move up or down as the sung pitch moves up and down. I suggest that the reader experiment with the voice to get the idea. Superimposing this type of a multiphonic over the "ring modulator" effect (see "The Scream" earlier in this chapter) can produce unique three- (or more) note chords. This mixing should definitely be experimented with as well.

Another excellent mix to try is the combination of the vowel harmonics for the low Bb in Examples 7 and 9. The procedure consists of buzzing (normal playing) one set of harmonics and superimposing the other set from the wa-wa mute. The only common ground between the two is partial number eight, and perhaps partials nine and ten, so the combined multiphonic structures are interesting indeed.

Is   It has a "sing-song" effect when the mix is done fast (see recorded examples).

The didjeridu (see Appendix III), droning on the same low F as in Example 7, emphasizes partials 5, 6, 7, and 8 below what is shown in Example 7 for the trombone. Then it doubles up, emphasizing partials 10, 12, 14, and 16, and leaving out the odd number partials except 9. Above partial 16, the didjeridu seems to give a full spectrum. These differences may be caused by the special peculiarities of (1) playing on the didjeridu's fundamental, or (2) working with a pipe that overblows at the

11th or 12th, or (3) both; but a plastic sewer pipe gives the same result. I certainly do not know the physics of it all, but the didjeridu seems to have an expanded partial range, stretching above and below what is seen in Example 7. This factor may explain why vowels (and vowel harmonics) are of considerable importance in didjeridu technique.

AUXILIARY DOUBLE OR SINGLE REED

One "multidivider" yet to be discussed is the use of an oboe or bassoon reed inside the trombone, or the substitution of a saxophone mouthpiece for the trombone mouthpiece.[12] Insert the double reed into the trombone mouthpiece and play on it just as one does on an oboe or bassoon (I rather prefer the bassoon reed). For some reason, the reed sound breaks up in peculiar ways not possible on oboe or bassoon, thereby creating an interesting and distinctive resource. Similarly, a saxophone mouthpiece can be altered to fit on a trombone; the sounds are of the same genre, even though distinctive. Composers would be wise not to ask for specific pitches or chords from these assemblages, since in the hands (or in the mouths) of trombonists, they normally lack control. They are also loud and often speak with an accent or not at all; practice, however, can usually control this factor.[13] Extended passages should be avoided, as using the reed is very tiring unless one has conditioned the required muscles; it also produces a back pressure and throat fatigue similar to that noted in the above description of double-stopped thirds. Some combinations with mutes, glissandos, vibratos, and so forth can be considered, but basically the double and single reed can create complex sounds which are excellent for imitating electronic music. Not too surprisingly, it creates results and problems similar to those found with the split tones and high double-stopped thirds.

Although a few comments have been made in this chapter about *combining* elements, the reader should keep in mind that this is a book *about* elements. It is not possible or even desirable to exhaust the combinations of devices; I wish rather to encourage the experimentation of these and all other elemental effects discussed. The voice can be combined, perhaps, more easily than some of the other effects in this book, but the split tone and double reed techniques will not lend themselves so easily to this. The key words are always *experimentation* and *discretion*.

---

12. The most famous, if stylized, example of this is Gordon Mumma's use in his *Hornpipe* (1967), for Cybersonic French Horn (an oboe reed in a horn utilizing electronic feedback). He has performed this work extensively in the Sonic Arts Group concerts, and it can be heard on Mainstream Records MS/5010 *Sonic Arts Union — Electronic Sound*.

13. James Fulkerson has achieved good control with this type of equipment and can produce a wide range and variety of sounds. He can, with his mouth, slide the double reed in and out of the mouthpiece, going back and forth from regular playing to double reed use. One should be careful not to swallow it! The single reed arrangement, by contrast, requires that one stop playing to put it on or take it off.

Chapter II:
Vowels and Consonants

Vowels and consonants imply speech, of course, but then the relationship of the trombone to the voice is not new. Indeed, the names within the trombone family originally were soprano, alto, tenor, bass, and contrabass, whereas all the other brass are named by key. Of the wind instruments (and the voice is included in this category), only the voice can glissando as easily as the trombone. The use of the voice in the trombone is significant, and, as stated in Chapter I, the voice and the vowels are the idiomatic elements emphasized in this book. Vowels and consonants best demonstrate the body as resonator and have a tradition of several centuries in didjeridu playing.

BUZZED VOWELS

Historically, vowels in the trombone can lay claim to at least some earlier twentieth-century use. The most famous examples would be in the trombone playing of the Spike Jones band during the forties and fifties.[1] The sounds obtained were simply u-i (oo-ee) and were mainly employed as a humorous gesture rather than in the more complex forms that will be seen later in this chapter. A rebirth, then, could be said to have occurred with the composition of the Berio *Sequenza V*. Here, voice and lip play several parameters (cf. Chapter I), vowels are used, and at one point the word "why" is spoken aloud without the trombone. Elsewhere in the work there are played references to "why," which breaks down into u-a-i (o͞o-ah-ee), and, coupled with the plunger (itself a "vowel" mute – cf. Chapter IX), this makes a very good "why" with the lip (see the two sets of brackets in Example 1 below).

IIa   The beginning step, of course, is to learn to produce these vowels, and one can obtain an a (ah), i (ee), e (ā), o (ō or oh), u (o͞o), and (to parody the grammar classes) sometimes y (o͞o-ah-ee). These sounds are produced by altering the shape of the mouth cavity and by changing the placement of the tongue. The a (ah) is produced in the so-called normal "bel-canto" tradition so elementary to western brass playing. The o (ō or oh) is very close to the above, except that the lips and forward mouth are pursed more dramatically. There is, through the instrument, almost no practical sound difference

---

1. Two recordings have been released consisting of reissues of these early 78 discs. *The Best of Spike Jones* (1967), RCA Victor LSP-3849(e) has "Cocktails for Two," "Der Fuehrer's Face," etc., and *Spike Jones is Murdering the Classics* (1971), RCA Red Seal LSC-3235(e) contains the "William

Example 1: Berio *Sequenza V*, Section B, line 7

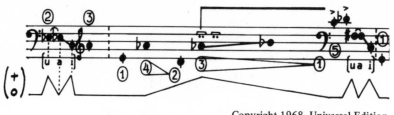

between a and o, so the composer would do well to consider them identical. The i (ee) is produced by a closed mouth, extremely pursed lips (with perhaps a slight roll outwards), and a forward tongue almost closing off the air stream on the roof of the mouth. The teeth should, however, remain open enough to retain good resonance. The u ($\overline{oo}$) is produced by a similar process to the i; however, the tongue is not so far forward and may be all the way back. The e ($\overline{a}$) is just the reverse of both the i and the u: the mouth is more open and the tongue more forward, although not quite so tight against the roof of the mouth. The y ($\overline{oo}$-ah-ee) is a combination of three more elementary vowels.

A number of pieces require vowels. Without question, however, the most extensive use of vowels so far for trombone appears in *General Speech* by Robert Erickson.[2] In his earlier piece, *Ricercare á 5*, the use of vowels is limited but interesting; however, *General Speech is* virtually a vowel piece. It is a speech, parody, or both, and nearly every vowel is used, as well as consonants. Consonants, of course, are difficult to really utilize, but a satisfactory approximation of them can be performed (this will be discussed at the end of the chapter).

VOWEL HARMONICS

IIb   It is possible to move back and forth from one vowel to another, and this movement can be a sort of waver or vibrato if desired (cf. Chapter V). When this movement is slowed down, one can hear different partials of a harmonic series, and the term "vowel harmonics" is thus appropriate (cf. Chapter I under "Buzzed Lip and Muted Vowel Harmonics" for a complete discussion). These vowel harmonics figure prominently in the didjeridu playing tradition, by the way, and are worthy of careful study in that context.

VOCAL VOWELS

IIc   Vowels can be made with the voice alone, of course, and the example (2) below shows how the vocal vowels are in juxtaposition to the lip vowels.

Tell Overture," "Nutcracker Suite," "Carmen," and others. Apparently the trombonist on most (if not all) of these recordings is Tommy Pederson.

2. Consult Vinko Globokar's *Discours II pour 5 trombones* for trombone vowels in French. It is recorded on DGG 137-005 (Avant Garde Series).

Example 2: Berio *Sequenza V*, Section A, line 2

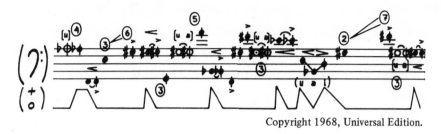

One can readily see how to make the vowel, such as u or ua, with the voice (see brackets) and then play it on the instrument. When playing, the mute is used as an aid to achieve these vowels (by moving from + to o), and the results of the two methods of production are very similar. In this particular case, the head should be turned away from the instrument and then returned quickly to play. This is wonderful practice for firming up the embouchure, since the embouchure must be formed on the instrument so promptly.

IId   Vocal vowels can also be sung in, or through, the instrument (cf. Chapter I). In Erickson's *General Speech* (Appendix I), the voice is used (through the instrument) to interject certain syllables. Usually it is the *en* syllable, as in "reve*ren*tly" (line 2), "wh*en*" (line 6), "leav*en*" (line 10), and "*en*tire" (lines 10-11). Also observe "*of*" and "*na*tional" (line 11) and "*in*" (line 14). The enunciation of these sounds is very important in producing the full effect, especially since they are so short (notice that "leav*en*" is the only long one). The play between the spoken and lip vowels becomes dramatic in line 11. Also, in Erickson's *Ricercare á 5*[3] the "ma-moo-mee-mo" section imitates, or, as the solo part says, "echoes" beautifully the lip vowels preceding it (cf. Chapter I).

Much more is possible with this effect, and it is the first step to consonants that are, in a sense, tonguings. The "m" (and "n") sound is really only the voice hum; as such it has already been mentioned in the first chapter. Vowels rarely just *start* but are often begun via a consonant or tonguing. An attempt will be made to sort out the various tonguings (or "articulations," if one prefers) and to point out that the various consonants are simply part of a tonguing continuum.

TONGUINGS

Traditional tonguing is a "tu" or "du," depending upon whether it is legato or not. It might just as well be "ta" or "da" (or "toh" or "doh" if the proper vowel were considered), and both tonguing descriptions are found often in traditional methods. The next step, of course, is to double or triple tongue. Many famous methods will have a "tu-ku" or "tu-tu-ku" (or "ta-ka" or "ta-ta-ka" or "tu-ku-tu" and the like) to represent this sound, which is akin to didjeridu mouth sounds.[4]

---

3. See page 5 of the score.

4. This whole discussion brings up the didjeridu (see Appendix III) because mouth sounds are used in didjeridu teaching to represent what the player is to do and what sounds he is to make, just as the mouth sounds referred to here.

Related to this, too, is the "doodle" tongue used in jazz, discovered by Carl Fontana, according to Phil Wilson.[5] The "doo" and "dle" elements are opposite to the "tu" and "ku" elements, which are decidedly staccato. In fact, many teachers point out that, when practiced slowly, the "tu" and "ku" elements must be loud and extremely short.[6] This is not so with the "doodle," in which each element is designed to be long and, so far as I can determine, rarely loud. What a remarkable difference in tonguings, and yet they are both sides of the same coin! "Tu-ku" can be somewhat legato (though it would be termed sloppy by traditionalists), but the "doodle" is preferable. The "doodle" tongue, then, has a definite place alongside the "tu-ku" double tongue and will undoubtedly increase in use.[7] There is, as yet, no common practice of a triple tongue version of the "doodle," but when there is, it might be "doo-dle-doo" or "doo-dle-lee"[8] rather than "doo-doo-dle." This contrasts with the "tu-tu-ku" and "tu-ku-tu," which both seem about equally hard (or easy) to do.

Most tonguings are adequately explained elsewhere in various books and methods. To complete the picture, however, a careful look must be taken at consonants, and the best medium for this is, once again, Erickson's *General Speech.*

CONSONANTS

Many western consonants break down into vowel structures. The word "ski," if it were spelled accurately, would be spelled as in the Japanese "*suki*yaki." This "suki" is pronounced in Japanese in the same manner as westerners pronounce the word "ski." There is no real allowance for the "su" sound in English pronunciation, but it is essential that it be taken into consideration. In the first line of *General Speech* (Appendix I), for instance, in the last part of the word "country," the "try" part is really a "*tere*e" sound, and a vowel sound must be added to execute the consonant desired. If all of these extra vowels were usually indicated in music, however, they would appear too long and performers might "sit" on all of these spots. In line 1, for example, at the point of "those three," the "three" being abstracted as "*thuh*ree," immediately following a "*zuh*" for the "se" in "those," creates a very different effect.

---

5. Phil Wilson, "The Great Jazz Trombone Stylists," in *The Instrumentalist*, February 1974, pp. 50-51. Wilson uses the term "too-dle-too-dle," but the idea is the same. I prefer instead the term "doodle" as used by Bill Watrous (and others), since both the "doo" and the "dle" elements are legato whereas "too" is staccato. It is accepted by most trombonists that Fontana has "the definitive edition," if Gerry Sloan may be quoted. Gerry also has recordings of early black trombonists using the "doodle" form of articulation, so it is not as new an idea as it might at first seem.

6. This was the case with all my teachers and is also true of various methods such as Arban's.

7. Bernard Schneider kindly provided information regarding early *legato* double tongue. He showed me a copy of Robert Mueller's *Schule fuer Zugposaune* (Musikverlag Wilhelm Zimmerman, 1902), pp. 69-70, where "doo-loo" tongue is discussed. If not the only published example, it is the earliest known to me, but it is not likely that Fontana or any other jazz performer ever consulted this method (cf. note 5, above).

8. The "doo-dle-lee" is attributed to Frank Rosolino.

A slightly different problem is noted in line 4: the "to" in "to build" is represented by a "tuh," but at the same time a "fake" D is played below the staff. A real one with the "F" valve engaged will not do here; the tone must be "bent" all the way down and back up again, an old idea often practiced by trombonists to get the "missing" notes above the pedal Bb.[9] This technique appears often — as in lines 10, 11, 12, and so on. Line 4 also has an interesting collection of consonants in the phrase "when courage seems to fail": the "w" in "when" and then "n" followed by the "c" in "courage" for a "ku" attack, the "juh" in "courage" followed by "ss" at both ends of "seems" with a long "ff" sound for a "ss(z)tuff" sound going into "fail."[10] Each one of these consonants attacks a note, and each one can differ from the others.

In my work with the didjeridu, the Australian aboriginal teachers constantly told me to enunciate (see Appendix III). So it is with this piece — the trombonist *must* manipulate his mouth to execute this speech clarity. A directive to composers: Do not hesitate to ask for clarity in speech performance such as this. It can be done (it is easy when one knows how), but Americans especially are guilty of speech patterns which slur. I find that I must continually work to execute vowels and consonants properly, although, it must be admitted, it has been far easier since studying the didjeridu.[11]

One more interesting collection of consonant-vowel structures appears in Jacob Druckman's *Animus I*, where the symbol ʧə kəts is used.[12] In the instructions, this designation "indicates non-vocalized sounds (loud whispers) to be articulated into the trombone. International Phonetic Alphabet Symbols used are ʧə as in CHUnk, kə as in CAreen, x as in German aCH."

Virtually any consonant, then, can somehow be approximated, and, though it might be possible to spell out every last consonant available, suffice it to say that some room must be left for the imagination. *General Speech*,[13] requiring careful analysis of the material discussed above and requiring attention to incredible detail, is only a point of departure. This chapter can only emphasize that point.

---

9. See the next chapter for a full discussion of "bent" tones, and also look up "privileged" and "falset" tones under *acoustics* in Robin Gregory's *The Trombone.* Larry Weed, in his letter of 11 March 1975, states that "Privileged notes which I call fractious notes (notes normally not on the instrument) were occasionally called for in (early) vocal music where there was not time to insert or remove crooks."

10. This "ff" sound is not unlike what is known as a "breathy" attack, except that it is in rather an extreme parameter. One may wish to look at the Berio *Sequenza V* and the Cage *Solo* to see other uses of breathy attack or breathy tone.

11. The first piece really imitating the didjeridu is the 4th movement of the *Concerto for Trombone* (1976) by Donald Erb. I premiered this work with the St. Louis Symphony in March 1976.

12. See page 5 of the score.

13. *General Speech* has recently been recorded on New World Records (NW 254). It is most important to listen to this recording with the score to understand how vowels and consonants are transliterated into the trombone alphabet. See also Erickson's *Sound Structure in Music* (Los Angeles: University of California Press, 1975), pp. 67-68, where the composer discusses the phenomenon of consonants in *General Speech.*

Chapter III:
Glissandos

Glissandos are of basically three types.[1] Two, the "normal" and the "bent tone," are "same partial" glissandos, and the remaining one, the "harmonic," is a "changing partial" glissando. Of the three, only the "normal" is the one most readers will recognize, since it is the one used in Stravinsky's *Pulcinella*, Fillmore's *Lassus Trombone*, and in many other works. Other examples of the "normal" glissando are found in both jazz and the symphonic field, and since it is covered well in standard orchestration books, it will be dealt with here only briefly.

NORMAL GLISSANDO

IIIa In using this glissando, one usually considers the positions of the trombone and also whether or not the passage will "lay" properly on the instrument; the idea is to have the trombone gliss stay within the limited augmented fourth range and not change partials. There are many instances of this augmented fourth limitation being violated, of course, and as one convenient example (1), the Berio *Sequenza V* will be examined.

    Example 1: Berio *Sequenza V*, Section B, line 2, bar 4 (large bar 2)

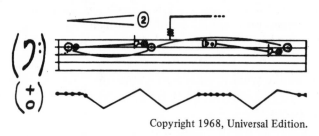

Copyright 1968, Universal Edition.

IIIb   Notice how the composer has covered the break in the glissando — that is, the change of position on the same note — with the mute. The change from sixth to first position is made at, or just after, the point where the gliss crosses the "F" line of the staff. Trombone players, generally, become adept at this, especially if the passage does not move too fast. The slide must move very quickly at the

---

1. See also voice glissandos in Chapter I and piano string glissandos in Chapter VIII.

instant of change; and the slower the overall gliss, the more successful that quick change. This effect can be accomplished throughout the range as long as the same necessary change note appears in two slide positions.[2] Even the "F" attachment can aid this possibility, but changing in the lowest range will not work as well (see a discussion of the famous low B to E glissando in the Bartók *Concerto for Orchestra* in Appendix V).

BENT TONE

IIc A bent tone is the result of a player taking a given pitch and, while retaining the same length of pipe (not moving the slide), lowering or raising the pitch simply by making the lip buzz lower or higher than the pipe will comfortably resonate.[3] The key word here is *comfortably*. Any pipe, no matter what the length, will tolerate any pitch; however, for the richest and generally preferred sound, a length of pipe in agreement with the desired pitch is chosen. A *bent* tone is the violation of this agreement. Bent tones are not peculiar to the trombone and are commonly used in jazz, having quite a lengthy tradition on both the trumpet and trombone. The bent tone is related to, and often coupled with, the half valve effect (cf. Chapter VII), and is one of the oldest "new" sounds on brass.[4] Jazz trumpet playing has used both phenomena separately or together for several decades. Trombone playing, on the other hand, has only had the option of bending tones, since jazz artists seldom use an "F" attachment.

Phil Wilson is no doubt the jazz player who presently performs definitive bent tones.[5] Often starting with just buzzing, even to the point of not really sealing the lips into the mouthpiece, he moves into the mouthpiece with a combination of a buzzed glissando and a bent tone. Usually, the trombone player's imitation of this old trumpet style is done via the bent tone. Phil Wilson has just carried it one step further in allowing the seal between mouth and mouthpiece to disintegrate occasionally.[6] Generally, bent tones can be used throughout the range on the trombone. Some players find it

---

2. One of the longest glissandos appears in Donald Erb's *In No Strange Land.* It is done very slowly and requires many changes to get from the top to the bottom of the more than two octave spread. One is urged to consult Nonesuch Recording H-71223 near the end of the second movement and also note the careful minor ninth tuning maintained between the trombone and the contrabass.

3. There is some sympathetic action of the throat as well (cf. Chapter V, notes 4 and 5).

4. Larry Weed, in his letter of 11 March 1975, states that "bending tones was a necessary part of Renaissance brass performance due to faulty instrument construction, lack of standardized pitch, and the problems with chamberchoir pitch. Hand stopping also allowed some help as well as pierced finger holes." (cf. Chapter II, note 9.)

5. The work of such players as Lester Lashley and Roswell Rudd should also be examined. See David Baker's *Jazz Styles and Analysis: Trombone* (Chicago: down beat Music Workshop publications, 1973), pp. 83-84 and 114-116. Lashley recorded with the Roscoe Mitchell Septet, and Rudd, who recorded with Archie Shepp, also has his own albums. Recently, the work of Dick Griffin, Albert Mangelsdorff, Paul Rutherford, and Eje Thelin have come to the forefront.

6. Wilson apparently developed this into his own style after hearing Vic Dickenson. See Wilson's article "The Great Jazz Trombone Stylists." See also David Baker, *Jazz Styles and Analysis: Trombone,*

difficult to bend over long distances; however, on the "F" attachment trombone, a player has the aid of the half valve option. Most players will find bending down easier than bending up.[7]

HARMONIC GLISSANDO

The harmonic glissando is like a bent tone except that the performer "bumps" over several partials. This effect is generally termed a "drop" in jazz, but indicates a rather specified use of the harmonic glissando and is probably the oldest form. It might simply look like this:

IIId

Example 2: Drops

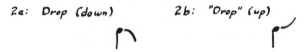

Example 2b exhibits a less common but occasionally seen version of this phenomenon, especially on trumpet. Both are methods of releasing a note and are usually executed fast with a slight diminuendo. Occasionally a big band will do a long, slow drop with the entire sections of trombones and trumpets together; these often are combinations of bent tones, half valve, harmonic glissandos, and normal glissandos.

The reverse of this phenomenon is the "rip," which is a way of attacking the note; it might look like one of the following:

IIIe

Example 3: Rips

Example 3c would not be as likely on trombone as on trumpet. This has also been termed the "scoop," yet this term can apply also to Example 3a or 3b. The term "rip" is more likely to be understood. The confusion with rips and drops is really in that *any* or *all three* — bent tones, half valve, or harmonic glissando — might be used. The term "smear," by the way, generally applies to the "normal" glissando but will probably most often apply to Example 3a or 3b. There is much confusion with all these terms but, in any case, all of these effects have been in use in jazz for many years.

What is new about harmonic glissandos is the extended use now made of them and the different forms they have taken. This increased use dates roughly from the time of the composition of *Bolos*, by Jan Bark and Folke Rabe, put together[8] in the early sixties. It was, for instance, a very influential work for Erickson's *Ricercare á 5*, and served as an inspiration for both Erickson and me to work on

pp. 135-137, for the complete written out solo that Phil Wilson played in "Flight of the Sackbut" from the album *The United States Air Force Presents "Serenade in Blue"* (Program No. 257, Disc 6, Side A). See after letter L for the buzzed glissando and bent tone, as well as multiphonics, fake notes, Tud-Ul tongue, and much more.

7. See the discussion in Chapter II about "fake" trigger notes used in the Erickson *General Speech*, and look up "privileged" and "falset" tones under acoustics in Robin Gregory's *The Trombone*.

8. By use of the term "put together," reference is made to the original tape version of Bark and Rabe overlaying the four parts (each of them playing twice).

new trombone sounds in connection with our collaboration on the *Ricercare*. Many techniques are common to both of these works, and several of them belong in the harmonic glissando category.

If one were to play the harmonic series in first (or any other) position by slurring from the fundamental to the top register, one would be playing one of the extreme versions of the harmonic glissando:

Example 4: Harmonic Series, Extreme Version No. 1 of the Harmonic Glissando

The expected form in these glissandos, however, is to move the slide from first position out to fifth or sixth, starting on the second partial. Beginning and/or ending notes do not need to be indicated:

Example 5: Usual Harmonic Glissandos

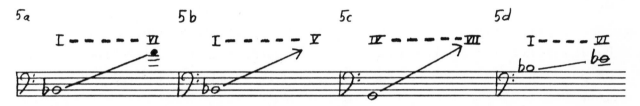

This position movement affects the intonation and produces a very rough effect. This rough effect can be further heightened by realizing, as one moves from the lower to higher register, that each change is accompanied by a slight downward "same partial" glissando, further upsetting the intonation structure. If Example 5d, for instance, is slowed down it will look like this:

Example 5d (bis): Slow Version of Example 5d

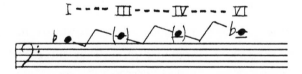

This slowing down need not conform to the above, for the positions may be shortened or lengthened easily. The harmonic glissando is, in some ways, more effective the slower it is done, but most composers seem to prefer the fast version. Also, all these harmonic glissandos can be done from the top down instead of the bottom up, but the latter is generally preferred. The advantage of the loud, fast, and upward versions is that they are rough and dramatic.

At the opposite end of the harmonic glissando is the ability to glissando harmonically on the *same* note, beginning with the E above the staff on up:

Example 6: Same Note Glissando, Extreme Version No. 2 of Harmonic Glissando

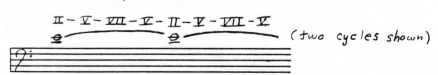

Technically this would not be a glissando; however, it is included here for some very obvious reasons. In performing the harmonic glissando on E, one moves the slide from II to V to VII to V to II while holding the E pitch as steadily as possible. The moving slide (length of tubing change) will take the pitch down or up, while the lip fights against it in order to change partials and hold the same note. On any common slide position chart, the E appears as the sixth partial in position II, the seventh partial in position V, and the eighth partial in position VII. A similar situation exists for every note upwards, and, beginning with Ab above the staff, one has four (or more) positions for each note, which is due to the closer higher partials.

The more slowly any given "same note" glissando is played, the more one hears the "same partial" glissando between each "same note" position. The faster it is played, the more it sounds like the trumpet player (again, usually in jazz) who presses different valves down (usually very fast) while holding the same note, very much like a valve trill (cf. Chapters V and VII).[9] Even fast, on the trombone, a "sponginess" of pitch is caused by these same partial glissandos.

These same note glissandos form only part of a continuum, which explains its inclusion in the glissando chapter. Shortening the positions just a little, one will not have the continuous E, but rather an E in II, a quarter tone higher in ##V, an F in VI, and a quarter tone higher F in bVII (see Example 7a). By shortening still further, one obtains an E in II, an F in #IV, a G in VI, and a Ab in VII (example 7b):

IIIi   Example 7: "Almost" Same Note Harmonic Glissandos Shortened

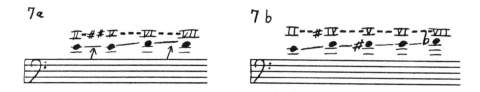

Shortening it further and further creates something like the version for *Bolos* and *Ricercare*.

On the other hand, if the positions are lengthened rather than shortened, one can get the E in II and the quarter tone below in bV. This works better higher, where there is a little more room to work: a high Bb in I, a quarter tone below in #IV, and an A in VI (see Example 8a), or a Bb in I, an A in IV, and an Ab in VII (see Example 8b):

IIIj   Example 8: "Almost" Same Note Harmonic Glissandos Lengthened

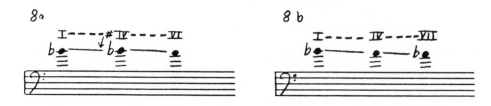

---

9. Double tonguing on the same note is also a similar and useful device (cf. Chapter II).

This latter idea (Example 8) is more difficult to do and is not as useful or as interesting; therefore, the practical limit then becomes the "same note" limit.[10]   This is appropriate, since the "same note" harmonic glissando is a desirable and extremely interesting effect (see the use of it in the Berio *Sequenza V*). In its slow parameter it will look a little like Example 5d (bis), except that when the slide returns, the pattern will reverse itself (see Example 9 done on a high Bb):

Example 9: Slow Version of a High Bb Same Note Harmonic Glissando

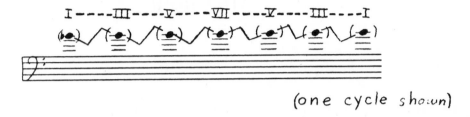

(one cycle shown)

The "exact" notations (Examples 5d (bis) and 9) are far too complicated to be of real value, and are not recommended except to demonstrate the subtle pitch changes that take place.[11] The beauty of all these harmonic glissando effects, I feel, is the "indeterminate" or "wandering pitch" feeling that they convey. They are easy to do, and to complicate the notation would make them much more difficult without receiving any appreciable benefit. Let it be concluded, then, that *all* the glissandos represent one of the freest and least complicated of all trombone techniques.

---

10. It might be wise to note that there is a similar extension of the limit of Extreme Version No. 1 (Example 4). This is starting a harmonic series in third position or lower and bringing the slide *in*. Since the harmonic series itself, let alone its extension, is not particularly useful in the concept of the harmonic glissando, a discussion of this extension is not warranted.

11. These notations might conceivably be useful in an extremely slow parameter for a special effect.

Chapter IV:
Microtones

Chapter III was a very extensive piece on microtuning, just as Chapter V will be. Both glissandos and vibratos are, in fact, made up almost entirely of some kind of non-half-step tuning. The slide, being unique to the trombone, makes any kind of unusual tunings or interval structures easy because it can be placed anywhere. Thus the title *Microtones* for this chapter does not tell the whole story, since definite interval structures such as quarter or sixth tones are not really "micro" in concept. Though this one word best describes what this chapter is about, its real title ought to be *Quarter Tones, Other Smaller than Half Step Intervals, Special Tunings, and Microtones.*

The trombone is unique in being the only buzzed lip instrument that can conveniently resonate any pitch. The key word here is *conveniently*, because other brass can do these things, but doing so is *not* convenient. Furthermore, if a trombone does not have a slide but is rather a *valve* trombone, then it is not really a trombone at all, because the basic principle which sets the trombone apart from the other brass has been removed.[1] To me, the use of the word "trombone" *means* that a slide is present, so a valve trombone is really a cylindrical bore baritone.

In the entire orchestra, the trombone is one of only a very few instruments that can handle microtones with real convenience, the others being the cello, the contrabass, and tympani. Others, of course, can do them but it is, again, relatively *in*convenient; e.g., the harp has to pick up a tuning key, valve and key instruments have to plan out their fingerings, on the violin or viola the distance between half steps is small, and so on. It is significant, too, that all easily microtoned instruments are bass clef instruments: Like the contrabass and cello, the trombone has a great distance between half steps. This distance is actually about three or more[2] inches along the slide, with plenty of room for pitch

---

1. "The simple mechanism of the lengthening-slide is, indeed, so complete and perfect that it seems to be incapable of further improvement, and it is quite arguable that a trombone ceases to be one when the slide mechanism is replaced by any other device" (Adam Carse, *Musical Wind Instruments* [New York: Da Capo Press, 1965], p. 251).

2. One should always keep in mind that the slide positions become farther apart the more the slide is extended (when any aspect of a tube is lengthened all aspects are lengthened). Most players become aware of this in using an "F" attachment but, oddly enough, the variability between half

material at any point along the way.[3] Quarter tones, for instance, will be about one and a half inches apart, whereas sixth tones will be about an inch apart. Eighth tones will simply divide the quarter tone in half, thereby being about three quarters of an inch apart. These are not difficult to learn, especially when one realizes that the whole step has been divided into half steps for centuries. Very complex intonation structures are accomplished with relative ease.

JUST TUNING

A number of pieces variously employ these phenomena, and it would be well to examine some of the notations involved. Of the more outstanding of these so far is Ben Johnston's *One Man*.[4] The use of microtones is extensive, even exhaustive. Johnston's idea is to convey a justly tempered scale, particularly emphasizing the seventh partial. The notation used is fairly clear except that it does not relate visually to the slide patterns. In mastering this work, I related to the traditional seven slide positions and used such designations as bV to indicate a slightly lowered fifth position or bbV to indicate a more than slightly lowered fifth position. ##VI was lower yet, this time raising the sixth position, and #VI was still lower, being only a slightly raised sixth position. While not quite as accurate as the original designations, these altered positions worked as a functional guide to the notation and lent themselves better to eye-hand coordination. After this had been achieved, then, using the ear allowed the fine tuning necessary to produce as the composer desired.

The only frustrating drawback I noticed was that after a few successive performances, where it was not possible to practice in between, the tuning gradually worked its way toward equal temperament. Only experience can tell whether this is a syndrome that will manifest itself in other situations requiring microtones. I think not, and would rather believe that this problem is caused by the performer's mind focusing strongly on not only "normal" problems, such as high range, but also those of theater and percussion as well.

A brief example (1) below will serve to indicate the problems involved, but it is strongly recommended that the reader consult the score in its entirety, for its interesting notation and copious annotations will be most helpful to any composer or trombonist.

---

steps is often overlooked on the tenor trombone. "The Relationship of the Slide to Pitch," Chapter 6 in George Maxted's book *Talking About the Trombone* (London: John Baker Ltd., 1970) pp. 32-35, provides an interesting discussion of this phenomenon.

3. "The trombone stands alone amongst the family of brass instruments in that it is by nature chromatic, and has never been anything else. Its tube is not limited to a fixed length, nor to certain fixed lengths calculated to sound semitones apart, but can be adjusted to all possible lengths within the limits of its shortest when the slide is drawn up, and its longest when it is fully extended. The cylindrical portion of its tube (over two thirds of the whole) can be increased by almost imperceptible degrees to nearly double its original length, and is absolutely straight except for one U-bend. Its chromaticism is complete and its intonation can be perfect, whether measured by a tempered or by an untempered scale" (Adam Carse, *Musical Wind Instruments*, p. 251).

4. Much is to be noted about this piece, particularly its use of accessory percussion instruments and the use of theater (see Chapters VIII and XI, respectively).

Example 1: Johnston *One Man*, page 6, bars 47-50

SIXTH TONES

Example 2, from Barney Childs's *Music*, is much more clear-cut. Involving sixth tones, the notation is unique and, although difficult to grasp at first, visually represents the actual sound.

Example 2: Childs *Music*, page 8, line 3

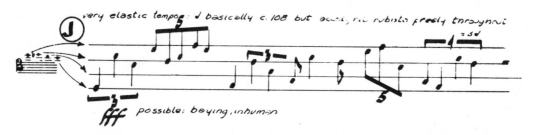

Each line indicates a half step (instead of the normal whole step), and this causes some confusion. The sixth tones are placed visually closer to the appropriate lines. A more easily assimilable notation could be used, relating to the normal staff, but would unfortunately take up double or more space in the music; for the purposes at hand, the above is a very elegant example. As desirable as this notation is for clarity, it has a limited range usage; how, for instance, can one express microtones with this kind of clarity in a passage full of leaps over an octave?[5]

QUARTER TONES AND EIGHTH TONES

A better idea might be the notation seen in the Ton DeLeeuw *Music*. In the instructions, he writes of dividing the half step into "ca 4 commas," further stating that "two commas equals a quartertone." The result in the music is a play between quarter and eighth tones, the notation in the piece indicating these commas. One useful aspect of this notation is its relationship to the traditional staff, and it is therefore easier to assimilate. Had the symbols themselves been written clearly, the passage would be virtually sight readable. His symbols, for example, are #, meaning a sharp raised by one comma (an eighth tone), and ♭, meaning a flat lowered by two commas (a quarter tone). An example (3) below will serve to indicate the ease with which one can understand and perform it.

---

5. This might never be a problem. See later in this chapter under "Leaps or skips."

Example 3: De Leeuw *Music*, page 4, line 1

MICROTONES

The most elegant example of the best "microtones" is seen in the Robert Erickson *General Speech*; one can observe microtonal playing from beginning to end (see Appendix I for the entire score). The microtonal fluidity of speech itself is intended here, and the notation used represents this admirably. The notation is within a traditional framework, and that advantage cannot be overemphasized because it enables a performer to assimilate the piece more quickly.

The true meaning of microtones is evident in this piece through the very fine gradations of pitch change taking place. The last half of line 7 going into the first half of line 8 seems particularly illustrative (see Appendix I). Notice how the pitch creeps up, drops back, and then creeps up again. It is this movement coupled with traditional pitches that give the work a sort of "sing-song" effect, a type of "sprechstimme," which is appropriate since human speech provided the material for the piece. Microtonal gradations are in evidence during the vibratos, glissandos, "fake" trigger, and half valve; see the appropriate chapters (V, III, II, and VII) for further information.

LEAPS OR SKIPS

For a workable notation involving leaps (all the other works cited have a very limited range), one should consult Larry Austin's *CHANGES*,[6] in which he uses partially filled-in notes to indicate quarter tones (up and down). This is workable for the purpose he has assigned, but how would one notate eighth or sixth tones? I prefer the De Leeuw system even though it leaves a question as to how sixth tones might be indicated. Also, I assume that any microtonal passage will generally be of limited range and large skips will be avoided. Skipping with microtones conveys simply an out of tune feeling, whereas it is the juxtaposition of *adjacent* half and quarter steps, for instance, that makes the use of microtones interesting. A notation such as Barney Childs uses, if it were expanded to a traditional staff (using lots of paper), or such as Robert Erickson uses, would provide the most useful *and* all-encompassing notation while at the same time retaining the relationship to the traditional staff. It is possible, then, to perform virtually any kind of microtonal passage. The examples above demonstrate that even the notation need not be a limiting factor if thought through clearly.

---

6. See page 7 (and elsewhere) in the score.

REVERBERATION

Using a trombone (or trombonelike instruments) in a reverberant room, or even into a piano with its pedal blocked, one can produce all kinds of microtonal harmonies that are of interest (see my *Ten Grand Hosery* in Appendix II).[7] The use of these is discussed at length in Chapter X, although one of those special effects deriving therefrom is really microtonal. That effect is the rolling of the bell on the piano strings, a sound that is very soft and, it should be said, ethereal. The sound appears in Krenek's *Five Pieces*,[8] using the symbol *ℓℓℓℓℓℓℓℓℓ* . Other uses of the bell on the piano strings appear in Chapter VIII and in Oliveros's *Theater Piece* at the very beginning (see recorded examples).

IVa

IVb

DOPPLER

There are two ways of achieving the Doppler effect. One is to twirl the instrument around with the player stationary, such as is done at the very end of the Oliveros *Theater Piece* when a garden hose is swung in a circle over the head (see recorded examples). The other method is to have instrument *and* player rotate as one unit (see the *Didjeridervish* part of *Ten Grand Hosery* in Appendix II).

IVc

IVd

In conclusion, the trombone is the microtonal brass instrument par excellence. Virtually any kind of pitch structure can be set up for use with a surprising lack of limitations. Having a completely variable pipe length conveniently at hand is similar to the ability of a cello or contrabass to vary the string length. Trombone and contrabass in particular seem to work well together, judging from the appearance of several recent compositions for this combination. The microtonal properties of the trombone (and other instruments as well, for that matter) have barely been tapped.

---

7. Also see Chapter X, note 11, for a brief discussion of my *Standing Waves*.

8. See bar 22 on page 13 of the score.

Chapter V:
Vibratos and Trills

The trombone produces vibrato in at least three ways, as well as in other ways that are more or less vibratolike in their function. Among the latter are the trill and the shake, which will be discussed at the end of the chapter. Of the primary vibratos, the variables of frequency, amplitude, and timbre, most instruments have a choice of only two, or choose to use elements of only two. Strings, for instance, use elements of frequency and slight timbre changes. Flautists and some double reed players use mostly an amplitude variable.

The trombonist seldom chooses to use a variable amplitude vibrato — the familiar "diaphragm" or "gut" vibrato — although it is readily available. The two variable timbre vibratos are accomplished by changing tongue shapes or by movements of the jaw. The former has no common name and is rarely used, but the latter is known as either the "lip" or the "jaw" vibrato and is used quite frequently. Also often used is the frequency variable known commonly as the "slide" vibrato. In jazz it is quite possible to find the slide and lip (or jaw) vibrato intermingled or exchanged. Here are the three primary vibratos, with possible notations, in their normal (fast and narrow) parameters:

Va   Example 1: The Three Primary Vibratos, Normal Parameters

1a: Slide

1b: Lip (Jaw)

1c: Diaphragm (Gut)

SLIDE VIBRATO

The slide vibrato varies the pitch by the movement of the slide,[1] and is heard most often in jazz. Example 1a suggests a possible notation for use in a song or a ballad. There is a large choice, however,

---

1. I have been cornered after lectures more than once by people who have apparently studied the slide vibrato in front of an oscilloscope only to find that it is predominantly an *amplitude* variable and not as much of a *pitch* variable as one might suppose. This is due, no doubt, to the fact that in the normal slide vibrato parameter the buzz of the lip does not change significantly but rather becomes a "bent" tone (and thereby loses amplitude) on each side of the tonal center. Whatever the point

29

in pitch variation and speed. In standard proportional notational devices, one centimeter will equal one second of time. The above example (1a), then, would show about four vibrato cycles per second. The example (2) below shows what might be done when varying this vibrato:

Vb   Example 2: Slide Vibrato, Variable Speed and/or Width

(Normal)   (Wider)   (Slower)   (Normal)

This could be written on a staff with pitches indicated (parenthetically) if desired, but one could also simply assume that the position of the vibrato on the staff would be the pitch:

Vc   Example 3: Slide Vibrato, More Definite Pitch Indication

The question at this point, then, becomes: "When does a slide vibrato cease to be a vibrato and become a glissando?" The answer is simply that the two can merge or divide at any time (cf. Chapter III), since the slide vibrato *is* a glissando. A special use of this glissando vibrato is seen in the Erickson *Ricercare á 5*,[2] where the note is attacked loudly and a quick diminuendo executed during a fast, wide vibrato. What is actually done might look like the following example (4):

Vd   Example 4: Slide Vibrato, Fast and Wide with Diminishing Width

Another use is the "vibrato" between the first and seventh positions in the beginning of *Bolos* by Rabe and Bark, a now classic example of how the slide vibrato merges in and out of glissandos. Shortly after the beginning of the piece, a wa-wa mute is "vibratoing" at the same time (see pp. 35-36 below).

---

of view, any trombonist who tries to play a slide vibrato with an amplitude variable mentality is in trouble! The point of departure should be one of varying the pitch; one must be able to blend into the normal glissando. It is perhaps significant that the slide vibrato can stop by use of the horizontal line and become confused with the "gut" vibrato (see Example 12).

In Andrew Imbrie's *Three Sketches*, there is a slide vibrato requested for the "dolce" section at the beginning of the third movement. In the louder sections it seems easy to make the slide vibrato grotesque. In the softer sections it is difficult to even hear the vibrato. In other words, the softer one plays, the more one must overdo the slide vibrato action; conversely, the louder one plays, the less slide action is desirable. This all probably has to do with the amplitude factor in the slide vibrato, since the "rate of effectiveness" of this so-called *pitch* variable is apparently changed by the amplitude at which it is played.

2. See pages 9, 10, and 11 of the score.

LIP OR JAW VIBRATO

The lip or jaw vibrato is equal in usage to the slide vibrato. This is executed with an embouchure variation — movement of either the lip, jaw, or both. However, the term "jaw" vibrato best describes the action: a slight movement of the jaw that changes the timbre structure of the note ever so slightly. This vibrato is the best one on the trombone for the purpose of "moving" the sound through the performing space.[3] The notation of the "normal" jaw vibrato (fast and narrow) can be seen in Example 1b, but it can also be varied like the slide vibrato where, in the case of Example 5, the extreme movement can almost pinch the tone off, or open it too wide, something like "bent" tones.[4] Compare Example 5 to Examples 2 and 3, where the slow versions of the slide vibrato became glissandos:

Ve   Example 5: Lip or Jaw Vibrato, Variable Speed and/or Width

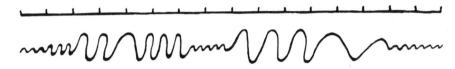

Mixing the slide and jaw is the easiest way to combine vibratos. The slide might be normal and the jaw normal except for being a bit slower (Example 6):

Vf   Example 6: Combination Slide and Jaw Vibratos, Normal Except for Slower Jaw

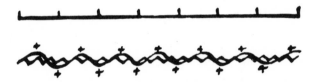

---

3. I remember the clarinetist Reginald Kell, in a clinic given during the mid-fifties in San Francisco, changing his vibrato so slowly that the sound would seem to leave the clarinet, move across the room, and then return again. When done normally (faster) the result would be as though the entire room space was the sound. Clarinetists generally seem to be more adept at moving sound around than other instrumentalists. Whether Kell and other clarinetists employ the jaw vibrato or the diaphragm vibrato or both is not entirely clear.

I have mentioned the jaw as being the thing that one should think about in performing this vibrato. In *The Trombonist's Handbook* by Reginald Fink (Athens, Ohio: Accura Music, 1977), p. 113, he makes quite a case for paying attention to the lips rather than the jaw! I would like to think that this vibrato is much more mysterious than either Fink or I have credited it; therefore, both of our attempts to explain this vibrato may well be oversimplified. To confuse the issue further, I subscribe to the theory expounded by Edward Kleinhammer (heard in a clinic) that the jaw vibrato is an excellent tone centering device. In any case, all of these factors, and probably much more, contribute to why the jaw (or lip) vibrato is so interesting.

4. The "nanny-goat" vibrato (associated with a certain style of playing that some band soloists used during the turn of the century) is a combination of "jaw" vibrato and "bent" tones. The "bent tone vibrato" seems to be a throat action, and therefore the term "throat" vibrato is not inappropriate. However, the "buzz" of the lips has to change, and it is difficult to tell which is more important (cf. Chapter 3 under "Bent Tones" and note 3). Also, be careful not to confuse this vibrato with the "natural throat vibrato" that Fink mentions in *The Trombonist's Handbook*. He states that "if you have a natural throat vibrato you should cultivate it rather than attempt to develop a lip vibrato" (p. 114).

With the superimposed vibratos (Example 6 above), designated by "plus" marks (+), the jaw vibrato peaks high and low once each second even though the slide vibrato is peaking four times per second. The resulting combination has an interesting "lilt," as though slipping back and forth. It does not take much imagination to see what can happen when these two vibratos are combined with more variation (Example 7):

Vg   Example 7: Combination Slide and Jaw Vibratos, Both Varied

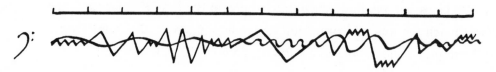

This is only the beginning, however. There are other vibratos yet to discuss, and most can be used in multiple combinations.

TONGUE OR VOWEL VIBRATO

This next vibrato is seldom used as a vibrato, and, while not considered one of the *primary* vibratos, it is easy to do and is also another timbre variable; therefore, it warrants mention at this time. It is the "tongue" or "vowel" vibrato, since the tongue is its primary formulator. Reference should be made to Chapter II on Vowels, since this sound requires a change in vowels by the use of the tongue: a-i (ah-ee). The i-a might be i-(y)a (ee-[y]ah). See the example (8) below for a notation of the "normal" tongue vibrato:

Vh   Example 8: Tongue or Vowel Vibrato, Normal Parameter

aiaiaiaiaiaiaiaiaiaiaiaiaiaiaiai

This vibrato is not only easy to do, it can also be varied easily. What actually happens is a change in the partial structure of the given pitch (cf. Chapter I):

Vi   Example 9: Tongue or Vowel Vibrato, Variable Speed and/or Width

aiaiai-a-i ——(y)-a —— i-(y)-a-i-(y)a—— i(y)a ——i-a-i-ai

The tongue or vowel vibrato is difficult to do along with a jaw vibrato because the jaw vibrato also harbors some sympathetic tongue movements as well. Conversely, when a tongue vibrato is used, it also has sympathetic jaw movements. Trying to do them at different rates together will not work properly; however, either can be combined with the slide vibrato (and also the diaphragm vibrato, yet to be discussed). Even though the tongue and jaw vibratos cannot be done together, they can be exchanged or traded off (see Example 10):[5]

---

5. Contrast this with the bent tone, or "throat," vibrato where the very act of performing it together with the jaw vibrato creates its special interest (see note 4 above).

Example 10: Tongue and Jaw Vibratos, Exchanging from One to the Other

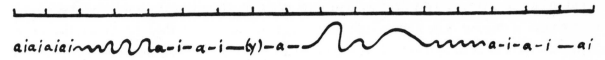

DIAPHRAGM OR GUT VIBRATO

The diaphragm or gut vibrato is not as commonly used as the slide or jaw vibrato, and, if used on brass, it would probably be used on the horn or trumpet, although it generally is not desired on these instruments either.[6] It is an amplitude variable and, because of its ability to be changed suddenly from loud to soft to loud, it has been given a "squarewave" notation. This sudden change or "bumpiness" may be what keeps it from general use. This bumpy characteristic, however, is well represented by the notation, and while the "normal" parameter is seen in Example 1c, its variables might be as in Example 11:

Example 11: Diaphragm or Gut Vibrato, Variable Speed and/or Width

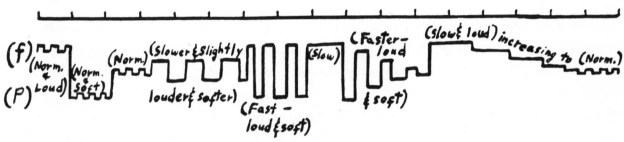

A better and more flexible notation might include diagonals (while retaining horizontals so as to avoid confusion with the slide — see Example 12). The slide vibrato, however, could also stop via the use of a horizontal line (see note 1 above):

Example 12: Diaphragm or Gut Vibrato, Diagonals Indicating Crescendo or Diminuendo

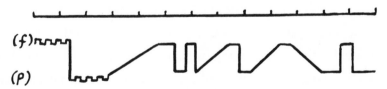

Just as the slide vibrato becomes confused with glissandos, the gut vibrato is sometimes confused with normal dynamic changes. Something like the above example (12) might be used in combination with the slide vibrato and the jaw vibrato as in the following example (13):

Example 13: Slide, Jaw, and Diaphragm Vibratos in Combination

---

6. Robert Erickson's *General Speech* provides good, if unusual, examples of the gut vibrato on the trombone. The usage is as much a theatrical gesture as it is a desire for a specific sound.

The possibilities are virtually endless. At this point one's imagination must take over to discover what can and cannot be used or what will or will not work in a given situation. One caution to keep in mind is that the use of three or more simultaneous vibratos can cancel one another out; that is, the texture becomes so cluttered as to be pointless. This is especially true if such other sounds as multiphonics are also being employed.

Many secondary vibratos are not really vibratos at all and will indeed appear under other chapter headings. The broader definition of what a vibrato is (or might be) must be considered; it is simply a motion or variation of one of three basic functions in music: frequency, amplitude, and timbre. Rhythm seems to be the only element that cannot be "vibratoed"; however, notice the rhythmic *changes* in all the examples. For the sake of completeness, then, the following phenomena are described (remember, the tongue or vowel vibrato has already been discussed).

TRILL AND SHAKE

The trill and shake are both frequency variables, and as such deserve mention along with vibrato because of the close relationship. Basically, a trill is a rapid change of pitch. Most orchestration books mention trills enough so that they will be dismissed here except to recommend that (1) lip trills smaller than a major second be avoided and (2) the positions of the trombone be checked to see that the pitches desired are within a position of each other. Extremely wide trills can become harmonic glissandos and should be thought of as such (cf. Chapter III). Wide trills over a fourth or fifth are generally the only choices in the lower register and therefore are not usually desired. However, a good fake trill of a major second in the middle to lower register can be accomplished by singing the required pitch above the played (buzzed) pitch (cf. Chapter I).[7]

The shake is another method (more common to the trumpet but still used occasionally on the trombone) to obtain trills. It is done just as the term implies: some shake the head, others shake the instrument, and still others shake both. These actions can be observed frequently among jazz players. I feel that a properly executed variable-by-buzzing trill is far superior to the shake. Jazz use of the shake, however, especially with the occasional coupling of bent tones and other devices, often can be important. The trill, however, is a method that can usually be more easily controlled and varied — assuming the performer is adept at it.[8]

---

7. Note the trombone parts in bars 43-44, 78-79, and 89 of Andrew Imbrie's *Three Sketches*, and see how, as fake trills, they fit in nicely with the overall texture of the piece. This work is recorded on New World Records (NW 254).

8. For a fine example of trills, singly and in multiple layers, one should hear the Erickson *Ricercare á 5* on Acoustic Research Record No. 2 (Acoustic Research, 10 American Drive, Norwood, Massachusetts 02062).

TREMOLOS

There are four usable tremolos on the trombone: the doodle tongue, diaphragm vibrato, the "F" valve, and the wa-wa mute. The doodle tongue (cf. Chapter II) produces a fine tremolo effect like that produced with a string instrument. The fast bow action on strings provides for the same sound whether bowing up or down, just as the doodle tongue can do. The diaphragm (or "gut") tremolo is not quite as good an imitation of the string tremolo due to its uneven dynamics, but is nevertheless interesting. This diaphragm tremolo is like the diaphragm vibrato (mentioned earlier in this chapter), only it is done very fast. When performed this fast, it seems to be a throat action rather than totally diaphragmatic; however, if the voice is allowed to vibrate sympathetically on the same pitch, it seems easier to do. The "F" valve can be used effectively for a tremolo and perhaps is the most interesting. It is similar to the doodle tongue tremolo except that it is more easily varied and can be very harsh. To perform the valve tremolo, the valve is moved quickly back and forth, much as trumpet players might move their valves.[9] When the valve slide is taken off, the valve movement produces a stark timbre change even on a unison. Done slowly, this effect can approximate a vibrato in feel, although technically, perhaps, it is closer to a trill. I have labeled it a "valve tremolo"; a full explanation appears in Chapter VII. The wa-wa mute tremolo is like the mute vibrato (as explained later in this chapter) except that two fingers alternate off and on the stem of the mute very fast.[10]

VOICE VIBRATOS

The voice, by itself through the instrument − or away from the instrument for that matter − can also vibrato by use of the jaw, gut, or tongue. Through the instrument, these voice vibratos create nice timbre changes and can be slipped in and out of easily. Inhaling and exhaling rapidly can produce a vibrato effect. It is much more difficult to do the same thing while playing, but inhaling sounds can be done (cf. Chapter VI).

MUTE VIBRATOS

Still other vibratos can be produced by mutes, the plunger and the wa-wa mutes accomplishing this best. Both are "vowel" mutes − that is, their characteristic sound is determined by the u-a (oo-ah) sound. This sound is produced on the wa-wa by movement of the hand over the mute stem and on the plunger by open and close motions of the mute itself (cf. Chapter IX under "Mute Harmonics" and Chapter I

---

9. Jazz trumpet players have for many years used tremolos on the same note by rapid valve motion. One of the earliest, if not the earliest, composed uses of this effect for trombone appears in Barney Childs's *First Brass Quintet* (1954), in the second movement four bars after cue #16. It is not a fast tremolo in this instance, but rather a "measured" tremolo in which the pitch is changed by a quarter tone.

10. An example of this appears in Donald Erb's *Concerto for Trombone and Orchestra*, at the very end of the 2nd movement. I suggested the term "Double Finger Tremolo," and so far as I know this is the first use of the effect.

under "Buzzed Lip and Muted Vowel Harmonics"). Rapid motion effectively conveys the idea of a vibrato. Two kinds of vowel vibrato can proceed simultaneously, the tongue vibrato and one of the mute vibratos; besides, the mute vibrato can be executed at the same time as the three primary vibratos.

Overall, it is best not to use too many vibratos at once. All of the vibratos discussed here work best when proceeding two at a time, with perhaps an occasional dip into three at a time. The interest comes in the *change* of vibrato *types*, and such changes can achieve a tremendous range and variation.

Chapter VI:
Other Body Sounds

By now the reader should realize that all sounds discussed so far are generally sounds from the body. The previous chapter concluded with a miscellany of various trills or trill substitutes, and the remaining chapters will move away from the instrument (the body) and into the resonator (the trombone) and beyond. Certain body sounds remain that do not fit into the other chapter categories, and it is fitting that this chapter be the "miscellanea" chapter, since it can be reached from either end of the book at about the same time.

BUZZED LIP

The buzzed lip produces the pitch and therefore is the most elementary form of the instrument. One fine example of lip buzzing[1] is in the Oliveros *Theater Piece*, to be discussed later on. As noted earlier, it is not necessarily the megaphone effect that makes a trombonist want to use a trombone, for that effect is only one part of its function. Rather, it is the resonating qualities and the ability to focus the sound that simplify buzzing.[2] Therefore, the trombone will be in use for the material discussed during the rest of this chapter.

---

1. See Chapter III, notes 5 and 6, regarding use of lip buzzing by Phil Wilson.

2. Glenn Bridges, in a letter of 12 August 1974, stated the following with regard to buzzing: "Few do this now, that I know of. Although there no doubt are teachers who still promote this for lip development. When did it start? At the turn of the century some teachers were promoting this idea of buzzing. However, Wm. Eby of Buffalo, N.Y. was the first to give it a big push, by distributing a correspondence course for all cup mouthpiece players — this about 1917. He created a big controversy throughout the brass world. He (Eby) was able to get many prominent cornet and trombone players to endorse his ads, etc. I was of course around at the time that Eby was distributing his course, but I never went for it to any degree, for I shortly thereafter in 1919, began to study with Joseph L. Huber who was a very successful pupil of Herbert L. Clarke. In fact Mr. Clarke used to say Huber was the only pupil that he ever had that really followed through on what he taught them about breath control, etc. Note the quote in the Huber biography in my book [*Pioneers in Brass* — see Bibliography]. It was the thinking of Mr. Clarke and many others that this idea of buzzing put too much emphasis on the lips and not enough on *wind control*, which really plays a brass instrument or wind instrument. If the lips are formed right at the start, proper wind control will make them vibrate, etc. I suppose this argument could go on forever. I remember receiving a letter from *Ernest* Clarke (Herbert's brother)

TONGUE-BUZZ

VIa   While it is generally understood that the *lips* vibrate to produce the primary pitch source, this vibration can be altered by a "tongue-buzz." In didjeridu playing (see Appendix III), the tongue sometimes is inserted between the lips to become part of the buzzing surface; the tongue becomes a substitute lower lip. This reduces resonance somewhat and creates a muffled effect. When the normal buzzed lip sound is returned, it can thump. Alternating the two sounds can create percussive effects.[3]

SLAPTONGUE, FLUTTER, AND DOUBLE PEDAL

The slaptongue is apparently usable only in its *continuous* version. In Robert Erickson's *Ricercare á 5,* I state that "the continuous slaptongue is similar to a flutter tongue except that it is much louder and more blatant. It is done by allowing the tongue to actually come between the lips and do the flutter."[4] Another similar sound that I once called a "horse" sound reminds one of what a horse does when it breathes out quickly with a rattle or flutter — perhaps causing its lips to vibrate. Although the term is

VIb   cumbersome, "tongue-mouth flutter" is a more proper name. In Ernst Krenek's *Five Pieces,*[5] I state that one is to "make this sound by putting the mouthpiece all the way into the mouth (behind the teeth) with the tongue flapping in the mouthpiece (similar to a fluttertongue without pitch)."[6] Pitch can change with this tongue flap by moving the slide. What actually changes is the "rate of tongue flaps," which slow down as the tube length is increased. This sense of pitch is increased even more by adding the "F" attachment, which of course adds that much more tubing. The function of this

VIc   "tongue-mouth flutter" can be like "double pedals"; that is, an octave lower than the normal pedals. To try this, one needs only to play a series of, say, D's starting in the middle or high range and playing all D's downwards. Near the end comes the "trigger" D and then pedal D. Follow this by suddenly putting the mouthpiece in the mouth as described above and do the "horse" or "tongue-mouth flutter" sound (with trigger engaged and slide positioned for D). It will sound like a double pedal D.

---

back in the 1920s, in which he said buzzing is old fashioned, so the idea must have been around a long time. Ernest claimed there were other exercises — such as slurring to develop the lip structure without buzzing, if lips are brought together tightly."

3. A marvelous bit of theater is the tongue-buzz done with the tongue as far out of the mouth (and mouthpiece) as possible. Although alternating in and out is not convenient with the tongue in that aperture, the attempt to do so is a worthwhile gesture.

4. See page 2 of the score. When trying to give a name to this phenomenon in 1966, Erickson came up with the term "continuous garbage," which was used in early versions of the score; it certainly is an apt description of the sound. I am not convinced that my term "slaptongue" is completely descriptive of what takes place, but it is close. The single reed slaptongue, after which this is named, is one isolated "slap" and, so far as I know, is not available in a *continuous* version. It is nevertheless the *effect* of a continuous slaptongue that is conveyed on a trombone.

5. See the instruction page.

6. A fluttertongue without pitch is just as the name implies. A normal flutter is produced (an "r" trill, or whatever), but no actual buzzing of the lips takes place. However, there *is* pitch to a certain degree, because if one listens closely one can hear it change when the slide is moved.

VId   While the mouthpiece is engaged inside the mouth behind the teeth, try the high, screamed "whistling" or "whooshing" sound like that of jet planes. This can be quite loud and a reasonable degree of pitch change can be used if desired. This high, screamed sound is begun just like the "tongue-mouth flutter" except that the tongue does not flap but rather continues to almost block off the air flow. Allowing a little bit of air to pass through at a high velocity is what causes this phenomenon; the more tightly the air is cut off, the higher the sound.

TRADITIONAL FLUTTERTONGUE

Perhaps a brief word should be said about the traditional fluttertongue. It is probably one of the oldest of all the so-called "new" devices and, if not the oldest, has at least had the largest overall acceptance. It has had wide use in jazz, apparently ever since jazz was born. While teaching at various trombone workshops over the past few years, I have time and again heard such comments as "Either you can or you can't," or "It is impossible to teach; one is either able to do the fluttertongue or unable to do it." The people who say these things are some of the most respected names in the trombone world. I am not going to be of much help here either, except to say (happily) that apparently most people know the principles of how they themselves perform the fluttertongue. Some say they use a tongue movement (and specify front or back), others say they use a throat action, and still others say they use the voice. One (or more) of these versions is like the "growl" (cf. note 11 below, and the information under "Throat Clearing" later in this chapter).

The fluttertongue is easily used in most registers and dynamic ranges. The only real exception to this is in the pedal note range. The composer, in particular, should keep in mind that any pedal note is *like* a fluttertongue; that is, the vibrations per second are few enough that nontrombonists often perceive a plain pedal note as *being* fluttertongued. Generally, a composer writes a fluttertongue to achieve a louder or more raucous sound. Neither of these things happens when the fluttertongue is used on pedal notes; indeed, the effect will be to actually *reduce* the very loudness and raucousness with which pedal notes are already blessed. For examples of this problem, see the scores of *Sequenza V* by Luciano Berio and Ton De Leeuw's *Music*. For the fluttertongued pedals contained in these works, or any other works for that matter, my recommendation is to ignore the fluttertongue completely and coax out of the plain pedal notes as much amplitude and crassness as possible.[7]

VOICE

VIe   Although the voice has been discussed extensively in Chapters I, II, and V, much has been left unsaid about it. For instance, the voice can simply speak through the instrument and the audience will under-

---

7. I find the *attempt* to perform the fluttertongued pedal hilariously funny. This attempt is in the best spirit of the clown Grock, to whom Berio's *Sequenza V* is dedicated. I am therefore somewhat undecided about what to do with the fluttertongued pedals in this piece, and often will try to both ignore and play the fluttertongue at the same time. This conflict may be even funnier than the simple fluttertongue attempt and, perhaps, all the more tragic.

stand everything that is said; it is a very useful lecture device. It is like using a megaphone but, contrary to the famous Rudy Vallee use for a certain kind of voice projection (not to mention timbre change and theatrical gesture), the use of the voice through a trombone does not necessarily mean that the voice is louder. Presumably, the extensive length of small tubing before the throat of the bell keeps it from being amplified very much, for on the tuba the megaphone amplification effect is quite pronounced.

Besides singing, then, discussed in Chapter I, speech can move from any kind of low growling to high screaming. A siren sound with the voice is easy to do — why not hit the bell with a ring or the mouth-piece to sound like a fire truck bell (cf. Chapter VIII)? Shouting can perhaps be more eloquently termed VIf   "quarreling," as in Example 1 below from Erickson's *Ricercare á 5*:

Example 1: Erickson *Ricercare á 5*, page 4

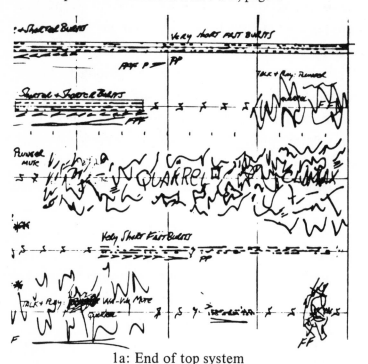

1a: End of top system   1b: Middle of bottom system

Notice that the second example (1b) is followed by a scream, and notice also the notations "talk and play" and "baby cry." This is perhaps among the finest examples of a notation that communicates to the eye a genuine feeling for what one is actually to do — or, at least, what one should convey. "It looks like what it sounds like" is one way of describing the best notation.

VIg   One favorite sound is the (dog) bark, which apparently first appears in the Cage *Solo*. It also is used in Krenek's *Five Pieces*, and many say it is heard in the middle section of the *Theater Piece* by VIh Pauline Oliveros where vocal animal sounds predominate.[8] Much more can be done with these tech-

---

8. In the Oliveros *Theater Piece* it is hard to distinguish particular sounds; therefore, this section must be heard to be believed (it is included in the recordings in the back of the book). When Ms. Oliveros made the accompanying tape for this work, she took live sounds that I had made and put them in close juxtaposition. It was soon realized that it would be possible to do most, if not all, of

niques, and it is interesting to see their development, as it depends on composer-performer imagination. These vocal animal sounds are not difficult, and they have a long tradition in didjeridu playing
(see Appendix III).

VIi   One more vocal sound remains, and that is the tight throat voice, which is a retching sound or an
awfully good copy of it. Neely Bruce, on the final page of his *Grand Duo*, directs the trombonist to
"play many obnoxious noises, as complex as possible, with interesting rhythms." In performing this
work, I find this retching sound necessary, combined with screamed double stops and other appropriate
material.

ESOPHAGEAL SPEECH AND TIBETAN CHANT

Next to the voice, two other secondary pitch sources hold promise for the trombone; neither has been
VIj   examined in depth, however, due to my partial or total failure in their mastery. One is esophageal
speech, often termed the "belch" method of speaking, which has interesting implications when played
through an amplified trombone (cf. Chapter X). The new equipment used by those who have had their
larynx removed may offer some promise as well. The other secondary pitch source that warrants investigation is Tibetan style chanting (or singing) through the trombone.[9] It will be of interest to see if
and how these things can be developed. I have had considerable experience with esophageal speech
(even though much dissatisfaction with the results) but very little with chanting. Experimental trombonists,
rise to the occasion: These research projects are "crying out" for the right talent!

CLOSED SOUNDS

Esophageal speech is closely related to sounds which I termed, some years back, "closed" sounds. These
VIk   are all varieties of tight, pinched sound, as the term "closed" would imply. "Stomach trouble," the
first of these sounds, is performed by pinching the lips so almost no air gets through the instrument,
all air coming from the throat. There is enough variation of this technique to allow a sense of high and
low, even though this is only a very raw form of pitch.

VIl   The same technique can be used to produce a high "whistle," "squeak," or "squeal." This, again,
is dependent upon squeezing the sound through tightly pinched lips with air from the throat. Actually,
for both the "stomach trouble" and the "squeal," air can come from the diaphragm too, but it is
much harder to control. Once one learns to do this, it is not difficult to *reverse* the air flow to inhale
these sounds; indeed, many trombonists may find this far easier to do and preferable to exhaling.

---

this sort of juxtapositioning "live," and that is the way the solo part has always been done. I was
instructed by the composer to study the gibbon (the small apelike animal) in working everything out.
In a sense, the piece (or at least that section of it) could be done "live" with three players. A more
extensive discussion of this work may be found in Chapter XI.

9. For further information one should listen to Anthology Records (AST-4005) *The Music of
Tibet — The Tantric Rituals* (1970). It is available by mail from Anthology Record and Tape Corp.,
135 W. 41st St., New York, NY 10036, and is well worth consulting not only for sound but also for
the extensive notes accompanying the disc.

VIm   The "kissing" or "smacking" sound is also an *inhaled* sound, surprisingly like the others, the main difference being that it is one short burst rather than a stretched sound. This is the oldest of these sounds, and was very popular in early jazz playing, especially on the trumpet. It is perhaps easiest to track historically on the Spike Jones recordings of the forties and fifties. One in particular, Rossini's *William Tell Overture*, is endowed with a particularly good example (on the trumpet) of the kiss, which is then followed by a "horse whinny" (a half valve, bent tone effect) near the beginning of the cut just before the horse race announcer begins his patter.[10] Another variation of this kissing sound

VIn   can be with the tip of the tongue, very high and soft, similar to the "clicking" that will be mentioned shortly.

THROAT SOUNDS

VIo   Related to closed sounds are throat sounds or, more specifically, the "throat clearing" sound. Just as its name implies, it is a rasping sound[11] in the back of the mouth against the palate, as one makes

VIp   before spitting. In fact, a very realistic "spit" can be simulated by this "spit preparation" or "throat clearing" followed by the aforementioned "high whooshing" with, perhaps, one "flap" of the tongue (see recorded examples).

        All of this is not to be confused with the *real* throat clearing sound, which is the "ahem." This is

VIq   perhaps best described by a "uh –– uh-uh-uh ––" but most people would know what was desired just by the word "ahem" (see Erickson's *General Speech*, line 16, in Appendix I). Some even use this "ahem" as a form of growl, but the "growl" per se is not discussed in this book, due to the aura and confusion that surrounds it.[12] In *General Speech*, just after the "ahem," a cough is required. Later on, coughing with hand over bell is needed.

---

10. Cf. Chapter II, note 1.

11. The "throat clearing" in the Krenek *Five Pieces* (bottom of page 11) is intended to be without buzz, whereas in the *Bolos* by Bark and Rabe it is written that the "German 'ach-laut' (throat clearing) should be articulated with tone production (growl)." By "tone production" the composers mean buzz, or normal playing. Bringing up the word "growl" at this point is wise, for while the growl often means that which is in the *Bolos*, it also means sometimes to use the voice in sympathy with the buzzed (normal) tone. See Gregory, *The Trombone*, p. 144. Be aware that there is much confusion about the growl, due to the differing ways in which it has been done in the past. It is a very old idea in jazz, dating from the earliest New Orleans Jazz. David Baker states that "Charles Irvis b. 1899 . . . d. 1939 . . . founder of the growl, played very 'junglistic' voice on the trombone – growled gruffly and suggestively on his horn, using a large bottlecap for a mute" (*Jazz Styles and Analysis: Trombone*, p. 72). "Tricky" Sam Nanton, with Duke Ellington, was probably the most famous growl player (cf. Chapter IX, note 5). Which type of growl came first is hard to say, although it should be kept in mind that the growl by the "ach" is the best sounding but the most tiring and hard on the throat. The sympathetic voice type is less taxing but more difficult to really perform; however, both types are heard frequently, as is another version done via a fluttertongue. To add to the confusion, see the discussion on "ahem" later in this chapter.

12. Cf. note 11 above.

CLICKS AND THUCKS

Ir   Various kinds of clicking are also practical. The "velar click" is the most famous, of course; simply bring the tongue down away from the back of the upper teeth while inhaling (see *General Speech*, line

Is   4). This can be blended into the "kiss" variation mentioned earlier. A "continuous velar" version, variable in pitch, is done by varying the mouth cavity with the tongue to one side of the mouth (see recorded examples).

Various clicks, thucks, and hissing sounds appear in the Druckman *Animus I*. They are rather well explained in the instructions for the piece, and a brief review of them will suffice here (also see Chapter II). The first is, again, this "velar click," expressed symbolically by a ⟨⟩ and indicating "a loud, implosive clicking of the tongue into the trombone. . . ."[13] My failure prevents its being heard on the accompanying record; however, in studying the tape part of *Animus I* one should get the idea. It is a fine sound indeed, and is the loudest of this type.

VIt   Another phenomenon is one I term "nonpitched pedal tones." They are not entirely *non*pitched, however, for a hint of the pitch is heard much as one hears it upon slapping the mouthpiece with the palm (cf. Chapter VIII) or the aforementioned nonpitched flutter. Therefore, the notation for this (in Example 2 below) is quite representative:

Example 2: Druckman *Animus I*, page 5, beginning bottom system

A nonpitched pedal tone is performed simply by blowing through the instrument with the tongue entering the mouthpiece to interrupt the air flow suddenly. The change in pitch comes by moving the slide.

AIR SOUNDS

VIu   One can simply blow air through the instrument making no sound other than the rushing of the air.

VIv   Various other kinds of breath sounds can be included in this category, such as the "dog pant," a sound

---

13. However, I have been astounded on more than one occasion by the amplitude achieved by the composer, and I find it a much deeper throated sound, extremely loud, and worthy of a better description.

which often creates a "whistling alternately with blowing" pattern. Changes in the mouth shape can produce all sorts of hissing sounds too numerous to elaborate upon. Suffice it to say that these sounds are replete with a rich timbre variation, as seen in the recorded examples.

INHALED SOUNDS

Air, of course, can be inhaled steadily. One can choose to have just the air, the voice, or the buzzed lip sounds. The Berio *Sequenza V* demonstrates how to breathe throughout much of the "B" section by inhaling vocally. Besides being a method of producing sound and getting air, it is also a marvelous theatrical gesture.

VIw

VIx   The inhaled buzz makes one realize that it is not the *pushing of air through the instrument* that allows one to play, but rather the *setting of air in motion in the instrument*. The loudness of sound is the same whether inhaling or exhaling. This is no less true of the voice, and the reader should try this while reading these pages. Breathe out easily while making sound with the voice, then inhale easily allowing the voice to sound again; the loudness is the same. In buzzing, then, the trombone is only an extension of the body. This extension factor, however, is basic to the study of the trombone, and certainly by now the reader has grasped its meaning. (For further "extensions," see Chapter X.)

CIRCULAR BREATHING

Another way of obtaining air is the method known variously as circular, continuous, or rotary breathing.[14] The term "circular" is the most popular, and somewhat descriptive, so it is used here. It is a method of playing continuously while breathing in occasionally. As one plays normally, some of the air is allowed to collect in slightly puffed cheeks. When the performer is nearly out of air, the cheeks *and tongue* replace the lungs for a second in expelling air through the lips while air is taken in through the nose. The cycle is complete upon the resumption of normal playing. Beginners should try this with a straw and a glass of water until the bubbles are blown steadily for ten minutes or more — and until one has quit inadvertently drinking the water!

This breathing can be done gently with no "bumps" or with a good slap of the diaphragm to give it a rhythmic beat (cf. Chapter VIII). On the one hand, it is sort of a "non-tongue" attack with the diaphragm, yet it is not a "breathy" attack either (cf. Chapter II); on the other hand, it is a rhythmic device. Just how one should categorize circular breathing is perhaps a bit difficult, but I feel that the sound characteristic of this whole device is the *continuous* sound and therefore belongs in this chapter of miscellany. Perhaps the most famous performer using this device is trumpeter Rafael Mendez.[15] The

---

14. This is not to be confused with the bagpipe technique. In this case, the air bag is kept filled with standard breathing, and the elbow pressing against the bag activates the reed rather than the player's direct air. Many years ago, one trombonist was known to have imitated the bagpipe, probably by circular breathing. However, this probably included vowel changes as well (cf. Chapter XI, note 7).

15. See David Baker's comments regarding famous jazz artists who have used this device, and also his remarks about composers who write musical lines that are too long (*Contemporary Techniques for the Trombone* [New York: Charles Colin, 1974], p. 219).

fact that this technique is highly idiomatic to the trombone and forms the basis of the centuries-old didjeridu tradition is not something to be taken lightly. The reader is encouraged to consult Appendix III on the didjeridu for further information.

Chapter VII:
Slide and Bell Disassembly

VIIa   The trombone, of course, is an extension of the body, and in that capacity acts as a resonator, just as we have seen the body itself act as a resonator. These resonators can change, and, while consideration was given earlier to body cavity alterations (as in Chapter II to make vowels and consonants), changes in the trombone itself will now be discussed.

MOUTHPIECE

VIIb   Several examples of using the mouthpiece by itself as a resonator or as an instrument appear in trombone literature. The first of two methods is buzzing through the mouthpiece, the example (1) below from Donald Erb's *. . . and then, toward the end . . .* using buzzing in the mouthpiece not only "live" but also electronically altered in the accompanying parts. In essence, there are five mouthpiece players playing at once, and it is a bit like so many chirping or flatulent birds, depending upon whether the players are single- or fluttertonguing. In the *Bolos* piece, Bark and Rabe suggest to "converse" but be VIIc "peaceful." The instructions describe this symbol ⊅ as a "Quasi parlando: playing on mouthpiece alone. 'Vocalize' parlando by working with hands in front of mouthpiece" (see Example 2 later in this chapter). In this piece, the term "vocalize" does not mean to use the voice, but rather to simulate (via buzzing) the rising and falling and vowel changing of a normal speaking voice.

    The second use of the mouthpiece alone is whistling on it, as one would do over a bottle. In Ernst Krenek's *Five Pieces*,[1] the performer is directed to "take mouthpiece out of trombone, cover big end with palm of hand, and . . . whistle over small end."

---

1. See the bottom of page 14 of the score.

Example 1: Erb . . . *and then, toward the end* . . . , page 5, top two systems

SLIDE SECTION

VIId   With the mouthpiece on the slide section alone, the resultant sound is like that of the garden hose (cf. Chapter X), and it can be achieved whether or not the bell section is attached. In the following example (2), the second player, with the "Outer slide off," is directed to "Play as pathetically as possible."

Example 2: Bark and Rabe *Bolos*, page 2, bottom system

Take instrument apart (removing slide from bell). Cover both open ends of slide with the hand, thereby creating a vacuum. Nimm das Instrument auseinander. Decke mit der Hand die beiden Öffnungen des Zuges ab und sondiere dessen Vakuum.		Stop: Pull tube rapidly out of slide, making a "vacuum-smack". Unterbrecht: Zieh rasch den Zug aus- einander. Vakuum-Schnalzlaut.
Outer slide off! Play as pathetically as possible without slide, as a recitative. Zug weg! Spiel ohne Zug höchst pathetisch und rezitierend.		𝄐 Even pulse. Gleichmässiger Puls.
⊳⟩ Stop! Unterbreche! ⊳⟩	Converse Konversiere Peaceful Ruhig	Increasing intensity ⟶ Maximum intensity. Steigende Intensität ⟶ Maximale Intensität.
⊳⟩ Stop! Unterbreche! ⊳⟩	Converse Konversiere Peaceful Ruhig	Increasing intensity ⟶ Maximum intensity. Steigende Intensität ⟶ Maximale Intensität.

STAND ABSOLUTELY STILL! AWAIT AUDIENCE REACTION! STEHN VÖLLIG STILL! WARTE DIE PUBLIKUMSREAKTION AB!

Reproduced by permission from Edition Wilhelm Hansen Stockholm AB, Sweden.

VIIe   In Krenek's *Five Pieces*,[2] the performer is directed to "take regular slide[3] off and engage on top tube only," which allows pitches to be varied by the use of the slide. Another point to keep in mind is that the trombone itself can serve as a garden hose by this method. In other words, it can be about nine feet long without a bell and with the slide fully stretched. This is the same as a Bb garden hose which, of course, has no bell either.

VIIf   In *Bolos*, one of the players creates a "vacuum smack" to end the piece. This is explained in the score (Example 2) and is accomplished quite easily.[4] Taking the outer slide by itself, one can blow over the edge, as over a bottle, to get soft, whistling effects (see recorded examples). Interesting dif-

VIIg ferences depend upon whether the other tube is covered or not.

     Finally, in this category of slide-alone sounds, the slide and mouthpiece are engaged together normally

VIIh and placed on the lips as usual, but with the thumb covering the bottom tube at the point where it would usually join the bell section. Simply moving the slide back and forth creates suction and pressure alternately inside the mouth cavity to cause all sorts of rather "bathroomy" sounds to emerge. No buzzing, voice, or "playing" per se is involved, and the sounds are not very loud; however, the results are well worth the trouble (see recorded examples). Some sounds are "inside" the mouth if the seal of

---

2. See page 10 of the score.

3. The term "regular" means to use the normal slide rather than either the tuning slide or the valve slide (the valve slide having been used earlier).

4. For years I have heard of possible dire happenings to the slide by using the "vacuum smack." However, no damage has ever been observed by me, even though this device has been performed on several different trombones. This is not to say that problems could not occur. Granted, if the instrument were very old and/or the slide were very pitted and consequently thin-walled slide tubes were a problem, then a performer would be a fool to try such a thing.

the mouthpiece and lip is good. When it is not completely sealed, some different sounds come out around the edges. Both have value.

BELL SECTION

Playing on the bell section by itself gives the shofar-like effect of a ram's horn or conch shell. Some players prefer to use the mouthpiece in the small end, but it is usually not necessary. Also, the tuning slide can be disengaged without changing the overall effect. Of real interest, however, are the different uses of the bell section while it is still on the instrument.

The Cage *Solo* is perhaps the earliest trombone work to call for a startling array of different sounds. This work was composed in 1957-58 with the assistance of jazz trombonist Frank Rehak, who "was excellent and that's why [the] trombone part is interesting."[5] Four sounds from this work apply to this chapter: playing (1) with the spit valve open, (2) with the tuning slide off, (3) without bell into jar, and (4) with the mouthpiece in the bell. This last presumably involves removing the mouthpiece from the instrument and turning the bell around so that the performer plays on the mouthpiece facing right into the bell. However, this instruction could also mean to remove the bell section and insert the mouthpiece, as described above, for the ram's horn effect. Item three (3), playing without bell into jar, presumably means to remove the slide and put the top tube into a jar.[6]

Playing normally with the tuning slide off is a little like the above Krenek example of the slide engaged on the top tube only. The advantage of the tuning slide disassembly is that, because of the normal slide still in use, the tube length can be extended. The result is therefore easier to control, because it is almost a full-length trombone without bell.[7] Time must be allowed, even more than in the Krenek *Five Pieces*, for removing and replacing the tuning slide, however.[8]

"F" ATTACHMENT OR "TRIGGER" [9]

By far the most effective device with the bell section is achieved with an "F" attachment instrument. This is because the option of the valve slide being removed is conveniently at hand while at the same

---

5. John Cage kindly provided this information in a letter on 24 July 1974. I then asked Frank Rehak to relate his story of this piece. Rehak's story, along with other information on the *Solo*, is in Appendix IV.

6. I also found that putting water in the jar is a nice effect, but that is another story (cf. Chapter VIII).

7. Putting the core of a toilet paper roll into the bell is another useful way of effectively cutting off most of the bell resonance (cf. Chapter IX).

8. Gerry Sloan brought to my attention a 1954 recording (Columbia CL 648) of "Hindustan" by the Rampart Street Paraders with trombonist Abe Lincoln making very elephantine sounds. I reproduced the sound for Sloan (Nashville, Tenn., 3 June 1977, during the International Trombone Workshop) by removing the tuning slide and playing over the harmonic series.

9. The word "trigger" can be assumed to be synonymous with "valve" in any reference to the "F" attachment, although "trigger" often refers to the entire "F" attachment unit rather than just the valve.

time the normal trombone is also readily available. This valve slide can be removed or replaced quietly by keeping the valve engaged, or it can be removed or replaced noisily, making more vacuum sounds, by allowing suction or pressure to build up by *not* engaging the valve. An example of the "pop" by pulling the valve slide is to be seen in Krenek's *Five Pieces*.[10]

VIIj   When the valve slide is removed,[11] the pitch can go through either the bell or the attachment tubes, depending upon whether or not the valve is engaged, and this option is available throughout the range of the instrument. I first heard of this device as the "cuivré," because of the sound passing relatively gently through the valve pipe and then suddenly being allowed to go through the bell, creating a tremendous accent.[12] It can be heightened enormously by the use of the diaphragm to give the accent or "cuivré" more power and bite. This is a fine sound for any instrument with a big bell, such as horn or tuba, and is heartily recommended.

VALVE TREMOLO

The term "cuivré," however, tells only part of the story, since it is only a small part of the total picture.

VIIk I find that the term "valve tremolo" provides the best overall description, due to its relationship with vibrato and trills (cf. Chapter V). To perform this effect, replace the valve slide with only one tube engaged so that the base pitch is a little lower, rather than leaving it off entirely. This makes the pipe length about the same as the normal trombone, allowing for the possibility of the same pitch, or nearly so, throughout the entire range on both sides of the instrument. This "valve tremolo" conveys the same pitch but with a timbre change. One can, for that matter, gain a similar effect with the valve slide engaged as normally, but the two pipe lengths are very different, causing different tuning: Both sounds come through the bell with little timbre difference. I feel that, although there may be a place for the valve slide to be completely on or completely off, the device is more successful with the single tube engaged.

The slowing down of this tremolo effect is much like the problem encountered when slowing down vibratos — it becomes something else. The valve tremolo was mentioned in Chapter V, since it can simulate either a vibrato or a trill, depending upon how the trigger is handled. It is much like the

---

10. See bar 5 on page 10 of the score. See also Chapter VIII under "vacuum."

11. See bars 8 and 9 on page 8 of the score.

12. I first heard this in the early sixties when hornist-composer Douglas Leedy demonstrated it. This occasion represented one of the few times that I learned something about new sounds from a horn player. As I concluded in working out the chapter on brasses for Ray Wilding-White's forthcoming book on *Twentieth-Century Techniques* (Holt, Rinehart, & Winston), most new developments have taken place on the trombone or tuba. It is of interest that, while the trumpet and horn have been accepted in western music to a greater degree than the trombone and tuba, it is on precisely the latter pair that most new developments have taken place. This tells a great deal about the so-called limitations that western musicians have up until now assumed to be applicable to the lower brass. It is significant enough, too, that the beginnings of the trend away from this thinking have come from Black people — the jazz artists on the one hand, and the didjeridu artists on the other.

"pizzicato tremolo" described in Turetzky's *The Contemporary Contrabass*, and thus I have adapted the name for use with the trombone.[13] When the movement is slow, it should be called a "*slow* valve tremolo"; however, when varying the movement, the tremolo should be described based on what will be said about the valve tremolo during the remainder of this chapter.

III The trigger, when moved only partway (half valve effect) and then back again, will create a timbre change somewhat in keeping with the jaw vibrato and, indeed, can be mixed with other vibratos (cf. Chapter V). Possible notations for the various parameters of the valve tremolo can be seen below:

Example 3: Valve Tremolo

Such an effect is well worth careful study by anyone, and a composer would certainly want to spend time with a performer getting acquainted with it.

If there are any effects that can be said to represent a *real* change over the last five hundred years, they would be the valve effects. Almost every sound discussed in this book could just as well have been done at any time during the life of the trombone. But the addition of the "F" valve represents the first change in these five hundred years.[14] However, it is not a *basic* change, for if the trom-

---

13. Bertram Turetzky, *The Contemporary Contrabass* (Los Angeles: University of California Press, 1974), pp. 7 and 8. Hearing this sound performed by Mr. Turetzky during the late sixties made me realize that it would be possible and, indeed, quite easy to simulate on the trombone. This is, by the way, only one of many trombone-contrabass sounds, and much between the two instruments is compatible and deserving of further exploration. Particularly, Donald Erb has carried work in this regard well past the beginning stages in his *In No Strange Land* (recorded by Mr. Turetzky and myself on Nonesuch H-71223).

14. Larry Weed, in a letter dated 11 March 1975, writes: "[In] 1839, Karl Traugh Queisser performed the David *Concertino* Op. 4 on an F Attachment trombone being developed by Sattler. Crooks and attachments to lower the pitch were known as early as 1619 (Praetorius pictures woodcuts with them in his *Syntagma Musicum*, Vol. II), but the attachments (Krumbogel and Pollettes) were for changes to other keys. The player could not vary from key to key as with the modern rotary attachments. Spring returns seem to be a common feature of valves from about 1811 on. Earlier slide trumpets (15th Century) seem to use a totally manual approach. [Regarding] double triggers — later work with Moritz, Wieprecht, and Sax produced a variety of valves, triggers, etc., most of which has to be further researched."

bone were to change basically, after all, it would cease to exist. The valve trombone,[15] as said earlier, is really not a trombone at all but rather a cylindrical bore baritone horn. Eliminating the slide takes away one of its basic elements. The addition of a "F" attachment is just that — an addition to an already existing phenomenon. The result is a double trombone, only one part of which can be played at a time. The valve tremolo, an accidental by-product of adding this valve to the trombone (see Appendix V), is unique and worthy of note, and is the first major acoustical possibility change since the trombone was originally designed. It is significant that one must dismantle the instrument somewhat to savor its full effec

---

15. This is piston valves instead of a slide. See Gregory, *The Trombone*, for further discussion of the valve trombone. According to David Baker, *Jazz Styles and Analysis: Trombone*, p. 54: "Arthur Gowans (1903-1954) invented a combination slide and valve trombone which he called a 'valide.' " One might assume this to have happened during the thirties or forties. More recently, various Holton Company advertisements show a picture of "The M. F. 'Superbone.' " These ads also state that this instrument "is a combination valve/slide trombone originally developed for Maynard Ferguson. It was his idea, really, to develop a valve trombone capable of playing ¼ tones without adding a fourth valve. Holton . . . took this idea and added a few concepts of their own [and] . . . developed a trombone that could be played with both valves and slide simultaneously. This means you can change keys easily without changing fingering, by depressing the valves and using the slide." (See *down beat*, 11 April 1974, p. 25, for a sample ad.) This may hold promise for microtonal playing and quick key shifting, but it does not necessarily replace the "F" attachment. One also wonders if an "F" attachment can be used with the slide/valve arrangement; it no doubt has been tried.

Chapter VIII:
Percussive Devices and Accessories

By now it should be obvious that both the Erickson *Ricercare á 5* and the Rabe/Bark *Bolos* are important trombone ensemble works. It is recommended that they be studied in depth for many reasons besides the incredible amount of material suitable for "trombone percussion."

TWO MOUTHPIECES

IIa   The first item examined in this chapter might have been included in the previous chapter. This is the effect used in *Bolos*, marked by a   ⟨symbol⟩ , in which the instruction page directs the performer to "beat two mouthpieces against each other." This requires the mouthpiece to be removed from the trombone (a disassembly) and an auxiliary mouthpiece (a percussion beater) to be taken up (see Example 2 in Chapter VII).

PALM ON MOUTHPIECE

IIb   Also in *Bolos* is a directive to "beat mouthpiece with palm (smacking sound)," and is represented by a   ⟨symbol⟩ . In the Robert Erickson *Ricercare á 5*, it is described as a " 'Tap' [which] refers to hitting the palm of the hand on the face of the mouthpiece [while in the instrument] to produce a sort of 'pop.' "[1] Both the "smack" and the "pop" are indicative of some basic notions about this device that should be taken into consideration.

---

1. See my annotations on page 2 of the score. When executing this "tapping" effect, be aware of the dangers involved. The main risk is that of jamming the mouthpiece in the receiver so tightly as to make removal impossible without a special "puller" which instrument repair shops have. The caution is, then, to tightly *screw in* the mouthpiece rather than allowing it to be put in just any old way. This makes removal possible by an *unscrewing* action rather than pulling out; indeed, it may be very hard to just *pull* it out. Only one case has ever been observed where this practice did not help. This was because the mouthpiece receiver and grip had thinned out where the fingers and hand touched it, the acid of this person actually having eaten through the metal. Since I have had considerable experience with problems of this sort, I recommend that before using this device, one should check over the instrument to make sure that the receiver walls are not misshaped. I have, incidentally, found a solution for those with too much acid, and that is to have *sterling* silver plate (as on mouthpieces) placed on the grip area rather than the usual *nickel* silver plate. Before discovering sterling silver, my acid even had eaten through chrome plate!

VIIIc   The mouthpiece can be hit by the hand in two ways, leaving the palm *on* the mouthpiece and bringing the palm *off* the mouthpiece instantly. The effect of the former is of a *closed* pipe, and the effect of the latter is of an *open* pipe. This distinction would account for the words "smack" and "pop," which imply quite different sounds. Both of the above pieces do not require critical attention to this sort of thing, because a variety of timbre is desired.

VIIId   Pitch variation is also possible by the use of either the slide or the trigger or, for that matter, both. It does require that the trombone slide be rested on the floor, the position changes being executed by raising and lowering the instrument. The distinctions and variations mentioned above do not warrant a full discussion, since they are too subtle for general application. They are mentioned only to make composers and trombonists aware of possibilities that could conceivably matter a great deal in certain specialized situations.

BELL EDGE HITTING

VIIIe   One more effect from *Bolos* remains to be mentioned: that in which the performer is to "beat edge of bell with thimble, finger ring or something similar." It is represented by ⊐ , another clear notational symbol for the sounds so characteristic of this work. The best part about the ring on the finger is that it is handy to beat or tap while playing or vocalizing. I have even used the mouthpiece as a beater in such situations, but this is not to be encouraged unless one has available an auxiliary mouthpiece of little value.

VACUUM

Other percussive effects can be achieved by pulling out or pushing in the valve slide to make a "pop" (when pulling out) or a sort of "thuck" (when pushing in). Both versions are done while *not* engaging the valve, but during the pushing-in version, the valve *is* engaged at the last instant. This works particularly well on long valve slides (such as on the tuba), so it is worth experimenting with on all the brasses. Related to this, of course, is the "vacuum smack" done with the main slide. See Chapter VII for further details on "vacuum" sounds.

MUTES

One mute used percussively occurs in the Berio *Sequenza V*. The "Glen Miller Tuxedo Plunger" mute is rattled in the bell, and the notation used for this is ●—●—●—● . Mutes generally cannot be used percussively, although that may be hard to believe when witnessing one falling out of an instrument onto the floor — a not too infrequent occurrence.[2] On metal mutes, a finger ring, coin, or percussion stick might be used effectively.[3]

---

2. One notable exception to this statement, by the way, is Larry Austin's *CHANGES*, where, on page 9, the performer is to "put down plunger on table . . ." at a specified point "forte."

3. How well I remember playing in big bands where the brass players used Latin instruments (claves, maracas, etc.) for Latin tunes. Lacking enough instruments to go around, a player might stand

STICKS

Erickson's *Ricercare á 5* makes effective use of percussion sticks. An instruction called "Rikitiki"[4]
requires a narrow plastic-handled percussion stick of the type that was used by tympani players during

IIf   the fifties and early sixties. The idea of the Rikitiki is to allow the plastic handle to *bounce* around the
grip area of the trombone. The pitch and the rate of bounce of this can be varied considerably by how
far into the grip area the handle is placed. This same stick is also ideal for use in realizing the "one
beautiful ding."[5] This stick has a rubber middle core, something like a soft mallet stick, allowing one
to play anywhere on the bell and achieve a variety of interesting timbres. The reverse end of such a stick
is also ideal for performing the beginning of the fifth movement of Krenek's *Five Pieces* and is also the
stick intended for the percussion part in Barney Childs's *Music*. In the *Ricercare*, there is also call for

IIg   a snare drum brush, which is very nice when used on the bell. Much use is made of "delicate percussion"
or "delicate single dings" which "can be hitting the tip of the mouthpiece, bell rim, etc., with the 'wrong
end' of the above mentioned stick(s)."[6]

IIh   Another beater that warrants attention is the "superball" beater, which is made simply by drilling a
hole in the ball and inserting a stick. The effects that can be achieved are mostly "rubbing" sounds similar to the tambourine roll done with the thumb. Another aspect of "beaters" is the trombone slide
itself. Whether a rubber tip is on the end or not, the knob on the end of the slide can be used to sound
various instruments, particularly a gong or tam-tam. The piano frame (with pedal down) is good too.
One should not do this too heavily, of course, for it might damage the slide, but the sound can be quite
good and the visual effect is astonishing. All kinds of other materials are certainly worth experimenting
with, but at least the essentials have been presented here.

CIRCULAR BREATHING BEATERS

IIi   Circular breathing, discussed in Chapter VI and Appendix III, provides yet another set of "drum beaters."
The diaphragm can be used to *slap* the note out. The tongue, tongue-buzz,[7] and voice also act more like
drum beaters in the context of circular breathing. This assumes a droning note, usually of low pitch,
which these "beaters" interrupt or alter. Another "beater," allowing water to collect in the bottom of
the slide, thereby producing a "bubble blowing" effect, can proceed simultaneously with the circular
breathing drumming; however, it need not be confined exclusively to that. It can be used at any time
and can be brought in and out of use simply by raising the instrument level, thereby allowing the water

---

up banging two mutes together in appropriate rhythms. I feel that it is probably the visual rather than
the sound factor that makes this of interest. In any case, it is easy to damage mutes if this is done to
excess.

4. See page 3 of the score (see also "Rikitiki" instructions on the same page).
5. See page 5 of the *Ricercare.*
6. See page 3 of the *Ricercare.*
7. See Chapter VI for an explanation of the "tongue-buzz."

to spread out evenly along the slide tubes. This "bubble blowing" and the resulting "pops" are quite substantial (further "water" sounds will be taken up later in this chapter).

EXTRA PERCUSSION

This section of the chapter deals with what I have termed "extracurricular" percussion. Most of this has little to do with the trombone per se, but it is possible while playing practically any instrument. The simplistic use of regular foot taps in *Elegy for Mippy II for Solo Trombone* (1950) by Leonard Bernstein, or the more complex and humorous footwork along with dropped mutes in *Consecuenza for Trombone Solo*, Op. 17 (1966) by Carlos Roqué Alsina are certainly percussive devices to be noted. Specialized use, however, has been made of "extracurricular" percussion by Ben Johnston in *One Man for Trombonist and Percussion* (note the use of the word "trombon*ist*"). It is a tremendously complex piece requiring a fair number of additional percussion instruments. The score itself is a compendium of thought for a trombonist in coping with unusual tuning (cf. Chapter IV) and many other problems, but it also shows how to handle extraneous equipment and theatrical considerations (cf. Chapter XI). The entire score is well worth study for several reasons. Example 1 in Chapter IV contains what is perhaps the most dramatic use of percussion, since it involves the better part of a drum trap set. This excerpt from the third movement requires the removal of the right hand from the trombone slide from time to time in order to play the cymbal.

Example 1 below, from bars 15 and 16 in the first movement, is performed with the tambourine, strapped to the right leg, either kicked with the left foot (first bar) or vibrated with the right leg (second bar). Notice the harmonic glissando, trill, complex intonation, and body turning going on at the same time (circled Roman numerals mean "F" attachment positions).

Example 1: Johnston *One Man*, page 4, bars 15 and 16

Used by permission. Media Press, Box 895, Champaign, Illinois 61820.

The example (2) below, from bars 23 and 24, is from the second movement. Notice how the performer must balance on one foot while circling the other foot to the side. Later on, the sleigh bells and tam-tam are used.

Example 2: Johnston *One Man*, page 5, bars 23 and 24

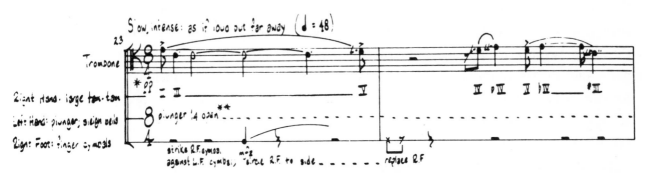

Used by permission. Media Press, Box 895, Champaign, Illinois 61820.

SCRAPING

IIIj The bell of the trombone can be scraped on several different materials without hurting it at all.[8] Scraping on wood, such as a floor or wall, is very good, the best being a wooden riser. This is no doubt due to the air space under the riser acting like a sounding box. Glass or chalkboards are fine, also. Sheet metal can be very good, particularly if it is in the form of duct pipes. Also metal and very useful are both piano strings (pedal down) and gong (or tam-tam).

Simply scrape the edge of the bell along the surface chosen to produce the desired sounds, holding the bell at an angle to control the preferred pitches. Different pitches are obtained, depending upon whether the bell is pushed or pulled and at what angle the bell is held. This will vary extensively with the instrument used; trumpet, horn, or tuba will each give quite different responses. When scraped on

IIk piano strings, all produce startling glissando effects. Because of the "give" of the piano strings, it is possible to "hit" the bell on the strings lightly. *Rolling* the bell on the strings can give a nice ethereal effect made up of microtones (cf. Chapter IV). Other resonators can include gongs and tympani. Also, blowing the trombone at these instruments can produce all sorts of harmonics and other effects. Large jars and bottles can sometimes be of value (cf. Chapter VII), and the most useful of all these is most likely a bucket of water.

---

8. I have discovered, finally, a small flat spot on the bell rim where most of the scraping has been done. Since it took about ten years to achieve this, there would be at least seventy years of scraping (rather continually) before much damage could be noticed. This would assume that the scraping was done in seven different places on the bell rim. The point here is to simply say that one need not worry about the bell unless it is one of those made without a curled edge. Discretion should always be exercised when executing an effect such as this.

WATER

VIIII   I have found that a bucket or wastebasket of water set upon a chair or table just to the left of the performer is most satisfactory. This is a tricky setup because one must be able to get the bell in and out of the water easily.[9] Some of the sounds available include getting the bell: (1) square and *close* (almost touching, but not *on* or *in* the water) to obtain a high shimmery effect; (2) partially in the water at an angle so as to get the watergong effect of pitch change obtained by dipping in and out of the water; and (3) all the way in so bubbles are produced. Another variation (on 3) is to inhale air through the instrument while the bell is submerged, so that some water is taken into the bell, then to play out with some force. A soft sound is heard glissandoing down as the water leaves the bell, then an explosive bubbling retch, or continuous bubbling if desired. Raising the dripping instrument out of the bucket is a wonderful climax.

Two kinds of water sounds have been mentioned before: (1) water collecting in the slide (earlier in this chapter under "Circular Breathing Beaters"); and (2) water in a jar with the disconnected slide tube inserted (cf. Chapter VII). The final water sound to be mentioned comes from a trombone in a swimming pool.[10] The trombone is perhaps the only instrument that can successfully be taken into a pool without damage, and this, perhaps more than anything else, attests to the simplicity of trombone design. There is simply nothing on a trombone to be hurt by water; other brass instruments have pads in the valves that would need to be dried out or replaced, and the water would affect the valve oil. Most trombonists, indeed, use water already (in conjunction with cold cream or something similar) in their slide lubrication.

KAZOO

Still another resonator requires special mention: the kazoo membrane.[11] Normally designed for humming, some buzzed lip kazoos were encountered in 1969-70. They were designed and executed by Kay Aiko Sato and Ronald Heglin and were made of ceramic. The possibilities for trombone (and other brass) are incredible; the membranes are not unlike the aluminum pie plates in the bell (cf. Chapter IX). Musical dictionaries refer to "Bigotphones" designed by the Frenchman Bigot in 1880.[12] These kazoos

---

9. With a trumpet, of course, it is very easy. The tuba and horn player have to exercise more care and agility in getting the bell close to water.

10. Perhaps it is the gesture more than the sound, but I clearly remember the sound of Handel's *Water Music* on a trombone while breast stroking (as well as I could) around the pool at the Oakland (California) Symphony Party in 1964. The sound was highly distinctive.

11. Related to this is the use of an electric fan. David Baker, *Contemporary Techniques for the Trombone*, p. 303, suggests that one can "play into a fan set at different speeds." This will not only be of a "buzzy" quality but will cause the pitch to fluctuate.

12. There were gatherings of "Bigotphonists" in Paris in 1910, apparently indicating a widespread interest, according to *The Oxford Companion to Music*, 10th Ed. (London: Oxford University Press, 1970), p. 108. Information about Bigot and his bigotphones is earnestly solicited, if not in time for a centennial celebration in 1980 in honor of this great Frenchman, then in time for a centennial gathering in Paris of "Bigotphonists" in 2010.

were often made to resemble trumpets and trombones, etc. But there is no reference to their being buzzed instruments. For that matter, there is no reference to them being hummed, as is normal with kazoos (see the "Buzz" section in Chapter IX on *Mutes*).

MOUTHPIECE BEATER

The mouthpiece can be used as a beater on the piano frame or rolled on the strings. It can also be used as a percussionist might use a metal bar on piano strings to produce howls and squeals, etc. It is better to do these things with an auxiliary mouthpiece, however, since a good one might be damaged. Keep in mind that, in the words of Lou Harrison and others, any sound is idiomatic as long as it does not hurt or destroy instruments. Care, then, should be taken of the piano used in executing these sounds. The problem of beating on or with a trombone is no different from that concerning a string player in producing *col legno* bowing. Sometimes secondary instruments must be considered for use, and the conscientious brass player should not feel guilty if he or she must use auxiliary mouthpieces, trombones, or other equipment. After all, that is what the bulk of this chapter has been about.

Chapter IX:
Mutes

The days of marking just "mute" in the score are, or should be, over. There is no excuse for this kind of casualness about mutes and mute timbre, for most mutes have been around a long time now, and much has been written about them. The standard mutes are adequately covered in the books by Fink, Gregory, Kleinhammer, and Wick,[1] not to mention many orchestration books and some instructional methods. Virtually all the mutes except the straight mute have come to us by way of jazz, and one can imagine the turn-of-the-century experimentation by jazz trombonists. Anything, it seems, was tried—most notably glass tumblers,[2] sugar tins, bottles, toilet plungers, and the like.[3] The plunger has since become a standard mute, as have the cup, clear-tone, hat, wa-wa, and others conceived in jazz to produce a unique timbre. Rather than detail the traditional uses of the various mutes, this chapter will deal mainly with specialized and/or unusual uses of them. However, keep in mind that no words or recorded examples can supplant the experimentation that composer and performer should exercise in order to learn about various timbre choices. No real difficulties will be encountered by any composer as long as the basic function of mutes — that of damping or altering tone quality — is understood, and as long as he or she realizes that, in dealing with mutes, there is much subtle variation even in the use of one mute, let alone a group of them.

---

1. Fink, *The Trombonist's Handbook*, pp. 49-53; Gregory, *The Trombone*, pp. 52-54; Kleinhammer, *The Art of Trombone Playing*, pp. 12-14; Wick, *Trombone Technique*, pp. 73-75.

2. Bertram Turetzky, in December 1974, recalled that he "saw and heard Jack Teagarden in Hartford (Conn.) in the 1950s playing (probably) *St. James Infirmary Blues*. [He] did some serious and expressive playing with the trombone [apparently partially disassembled] and a whiskey glass." It could be presumed to have been the slide section alone with the glass held over the pipe, or else held over the pipe where the tuning slide would normally be. See also Baker's comment on Charles Irvis in Chapter VI, note 11, above.

3. Gerry Sloan pointed out to me that much material can be noted in the article "Muted Brass" by Keith Nichols, in *Storyville* No. 30 (August-September, 1970), pp. 203-206. Nichols points out that one of the primary uses of the mutes, particularly the straight mute, was to cope with the fact that early recording techniques were generally unable to deal with the open horn sound due to the amplitude. The whole style trend of commercial bands using continual muting may have had its origin in dealing with this recording problem.

WA-WA

The subtle differences in one mute can be absolutely astounding. To convey the idea, the mute most likely to arouse this kind of curiosity will be discussed, and that is the wa-wa, otherwise known as the Harmon, after the company that manufactures them. It is called a wa-wa from its ability to make that ua (oo-ah) vowel sound discussed in Chapter II; the uauaua that is so familiar can be seen in more detail in Chapter V on the vibrato. The left hand is placed over the stem for the 'u' and opened up for the

IXa 'a,' this generally assuming that the stem of the mute is pushed in all the way (although this can be
IXb done with it pulled out any distance: see recorded examples). The term "stem out" does not mean to
IXc remove the stem (though this can also be done), but rather to pull the stem to its full length.[4] Fink
IXd describes the wa-wa mute stem as being with and without the "cookie cutter," depending upon what era the music is from. The earlier the music, the more likely the "cookie cutter" is left on the stem of the mute. Since 1950 this seems not to be the case, according to Fink. However, in contemporary avant garde music it is the ua effect that is desired, and this would mean that the "cookie cutter" *is* left on the stem, even since 1950, at least for the so-called avant garde style.

BUZZ

Each mute is practically a separate instrument, and perhaps the wa-wa is the best vehicle to emphasize this point. When, in 1964, I first encountered the Cage *Solo*, I was confronted with the term "buzz"

IXe mute. The "buzziest" sound that was to be found was the wa-wa mute held backwards gently against the bell, which produced a terrific rattling. Similar effects, since discovered, can be achieved with aluminum pie plates held over the bell. They can even be controlled by putting a finger in various places on the plate — like producing harmonics on cymbals — and these "harmonics" can be changed quickly by putting different fingers down. Quite a variation can be achieved by using different sizes of plates (see the next section on "Plunger" and also the section on "Kazoo" in Chapter VIII). For that matter, one can simply buzz with the lips *through* the wa-wa.[5]

---

4. A muting problem had to be solved with the Ton De Leeuw *Music*. With about ten days to learn the piece for its premiere (5 June 1974 at Peabody College for Teachers in Nashville, Tennessee, during the fourth annual International Trombone Workshop), and no time for questions to the composer, an answer had to be found for, among other things, the directive of "sharp mute" on page 6 of the score. Two hours of thought and experimentation determined (wrongly, perhaps) that (1) by the composer's use of the term "sharp" he meant "edgy" or "harsh" or "brittle" or any combination thereof, and that (2) the wa-wa with maximally extended stem would best convey this. This is an example of how the trombonist must be constantly ready to experiment; wrong or incomplete mute directions, while of the grossest oversights of composition, seem to be the norm. This is due, no doubt, to the fact that there has not been much sensitivity to mute timbre differences until very recently; but in any case, I was happy to have received even as much information in that score as I did.

5. Cf. Chapter VIII, note 11, regarding use of an electric fan. Also, in listening to jug band recordings, one will note the buzzing over the top of jugs, the jug serving simply as a resonator. Gerry Sloan showed me various pictures of Dickie Wells using his "pepper-pot" mute — a straight mute with many holes in it. One picture, the one on the album by Dickie Wells All Stars called *Bone Four-in-Hand* (MJR 8118) shows him using it (possibly) inserted backwards. This would be similar to the wa-wa

PLUNGER

IXf   The plunger is another mute upon which it is possible to buzz, which is achieved when the mute is tightly closed into the bell. The term for this is "tight plunger"; however, I happily found out[6] that if a hole is cut in the center of the plunger, a whole range of tight plunger effects is available. Oddly enough, the regular "tight" position does not work very well when this hole is made, although a finger can easily be inserted to plug it up. The interest with the hole is in pressing the center of the plunger as far into the bell as possible. This requires a relatively new plunger, since old ones get stiff and do not flex as well. The farther in it is pressed, the more prominent and "buzzy" the high partials become. The plunger, like the wa-wa, produces a ua (oo-ah) when opened and closed. The main advantages of the plunger mute over *all* the others are its low cost and the availability of the open horn option constantly at hand. The mute referred to here is the conventional toilet plunger; however, for the Berio *Sequenza V*, Alsina's *Consecuenza*, and other works of similar difficulty, it is wise to use the "Glen Miller Tuxedo Plunger" mute[7] or the "wow-wow" mute.[8] These are elegant forms of the rubber plunger and the tuning is easier to control. These mutes, by the way, may also be used percussively (cf. Chapter VIII).[9]

IXg   There is a combined buzz and ua accomplished by placing a trumpet straight mute as far into the bell as it will go and then manipulating a plunger over it.[10] The convenient open horn option is not available with this combination, but it nevertheless is a very important and unique device (see recorded examples).

---

used backwards as cited above. However, it may be more than likely that he has it handy for a quick insertion the normal way. Sloan also brought to my attention Duke Ellington's comment in his *Music Is My Mistress* (New York: Doubleday, 1973) p. 108: "Before Tricky joined us, Charles Irvis [cf. Chapter VI, note 11], who was known as Charlie Plug, was our original trombone player down in the Kentucky Club. He was called Plug because of the device he used on his horn. In those days they manufactured a kind of mute designed to make the trombone sound like a saxophone. The sax was still regarded as new then. Charlie had dropped this device and broken it, so he used what was left of it, rolling it around the bell of his trombone. He couldn't use it the way it was intended, because of the part broken off, but he'd get this entirely different, lecherous, low tone, and no one has ever done it since. You might say that there was really a lost art."

6. Thanks to Buddy Baker.

7. Manufactured by Humes and Berg.

8. Manufactured by Harmon.

9. When first working on *Sequenza V*, I was unable to ascertain from the composer just which mute was intended, the instruction "metal mute" being incorrect or, at the very least, incomplete. I used a rubber plunger mute with thumbtacks around the edge for the "rattling" (cf. Chapter VIII) for about two years (1966-68).

10. David Baker, in his *Contemporary Techniques for the Trombone*, p. 312, states that "the plunger is often used with a shortened [trombone] straight mute." I estimate that this combination use dates from around the twenties. I discovered this technique in the early fifties when trying to determine what Pee-wee Hunt was up to on his 78 RPM Capitol Records release of *Sugar Blues*.

HAT

Xh   The hat mute — a derby or its manufactured counterparts of fibre or metal — also has the open horn

option available. It has a further advantage in that it may conveniently be mounted on a stand, and

therefore no hands are needed to manipulate it; however, when a stand is used, it is more difficult to

get the kind of rapid open (o) to closed (+) sound so often desired from these kinds of mutes. This

mute, as it turns out, is hard for a trombonist to manipulate by hand anyway (thus it does not appear

in the vibrato chapter).[11] Having the left hand free to manipulate the "F" attachment can be of great

value, because situations have arisen in which the left hand was manipulating a wa-wa or plunger while at

the same time trigger notes were called for. This is an easy mistake to make, and composers should be

aware of this relatively new problem.

FELT, BUCKET, AND HAND

A somewhat similar effect to the hat can be achieved by placing a piece of felt over the bell. Draping a

chamois over the bell, or even using the center from an old felt hat, can achieve a useful damping effect

IXi   much like the velvetone or "bucket" mute (which is often dubbed a "can-o'-rags").[12] Even the hand

over the bell can approximate this, but it is hard to get the hand in the bell far enough to get a completely

covered sound and still play! Fink has good descriptions complete with photographs of what to do with

the hand. His mention of the term "quasi horn," a typical directive found in jazz or studio scores, indi-

cates the effect desired.

The damping effect may be better achieved by use of a toilet paper core inserted into the bell. Bergsma

uses this effect, which is the first use so far as I know, in his *Blatant Hypotheses for Trombone and Per-

cussion* (1977). In the second movement, he wanted an extremely soft and delicate sound, and he liked

the idea of the covered effect that the toilet paper core gave to the trombone tone. Bergsma further

heightened the interest by the occasional use of the plunger along with the toilet paper core.

A toilet paper core inserted into the bell produces the effect of a cut-off bell, much like the sound

that the very early trombones (sackbuts) must have had. For this reason, I have found it wise to use this

device when playing with other instruments of the sixteenth century. Granted, it would be preferable

to use a sixteenth-century trombone, or a copy of one, but these are not always obtainable. The use of

the toilet paper core is cheap, instant, and not visually disturbing, with only a small amount of peculiar

intonation to deal with — no more so, actually, than that which would be encountered with an old

---

11. Robert Suderburg's *Chamber Music III* (1971), in the "It's been a long, long time" (second)
movement, makes extensive use of the hat mute. This piece, which is reflective of the muted dance
bands of the thirties, shows this mute to be a visual as well as an acoustical symbol of that era. This
work will soon be released on Columbia Records.

12. The plunger can imitate the bucket mute if the side of the plunger is bent in a little and held
away from the bell at a slight angle. A fine bucket mute is now made by Jerry Finch (P.O. Box 631,
Chula Vista, CA 92012) and is called the "Finch" mute. It is sturdy, lightweight, and can be installed
or removed with one hand. One is cautioned to specify instrument make and model and submit a
bell tracing in order to receive the proper size.

instrument. For that matter, the use of *any* mute creates tuning problems that any experienced brass player is used to solving.

CUP

Unless one is firmly ensconced in dance and studio work or playing in pops orchestras, an investment in a cup mute for trombone may not be necessarily worthwhile. The cup, while a standard on trumpet, is perhaps the most finicky of all the trombone mutes, mostly because just any cup does not fit just any trombone. Although *supposedly* a standard, the cup mute provides more complications than the wa-wa, but, fortunately, contemporary composers find the latter more to their liking. The cup simply does not have the convenience or the wide range of effects.

IXj   Cup mutes generally have an open, half open, or "tight cup" (closed) option. "Tight cup" is a directive often found in dance band music, and it is presumed that the mute was made to fit tight and no other way unless two mutes were carried around.[13] The tight cup effect, however, can perhaps be just as easily done on a "whisper" mute,[14] a mute made for practicing and one more likely to fit different bells. Also, a mic-a-mute[15] can be considered, but it is shaped like the cup and has the same fitting problem. It can also be imitated by a bucket or felt.

In a piece calling for several trombones with cup mutes, problems result even assuming that all players have these mutes (which they might not). The cups never fit the same way in the different sized bells, and any approximation would be a major undertaking. One company[16] is now making mutes with adjustable (sliding) cups, but those cups that are more commonly available are made of many different materials. In contrast, wa-wa mutes are almost all metal and, if they need to be adapted for a bigger bell size, need only a larger cork. There is no risk of sound change. It is hoped that, with the return of the sliding cup mute, the beautiful sound variation possible with cup mutes can become part of the mute nucleus — or, at least, a recommended accessory to it.

---

13. It is my good fortune to be blessed with an old cup mute especially made by the late Frank DePolis of Philadelphia in about 1956 on which the cup part can slide along the straight shank. Presumably it was designed to adjust to different bell sizes, but I found the option of "tight" or "open" cup to be possible in an instant (see recorded examples). Recently it has been discovered that Accura Music (Box 887, Athens, Ohio 45701) is making adjustable cups along the lines of the DePolis mute. There are two sizes (for large tenor and for bass trombone), and if these become really popular they could go a long way toward bringing the cup mute back into more general circulation.

14. Actually this is a "Whispa-mute" made by Charlie Spivak. This is one to experiment with for extremely quiet sounds.

15. Manufactured by Humes and Berg.

16. See note 13 above.

MUTE NUCLEUS

In any score, the directive "mute" is always assumed to be a straight mute; but since these mutes are so variable, several different straights of fibre, metal, wood, etc., are advised in order to adjust to conductor or composer requests. A trombonist, then, should own a plunger (or several plungers), a wa-wa, felt, and several straight mutes as a basic nucleus. Even in contemporary music, ninety percent of mute requirements will call for mutes among these four. The expensive mutes among them are the wa-wa and all the straight mutes; however, one would be expected to own straight mutes anyway for any kind of traditional playing. The right straight mute can be really important. Anton Webern, for instance, conceived of the trombone as *being* no other way but with a straight mute; one need only examine his works. However, realizing what a sensitive man Webern was with regard to timbre, I wonder what sound from all the straights available he really wanted.[17]

The four mutes mentioned — the straight, plunger, felt, and wa-wa — are a recommended nucleus because of their consistency; that is, if a composer asks for any one of these four, there is usually no question in the mind of *either* the composer *or* the performer as to the sound desired. When it comes to cups, bucket, hat, clear-tone (solo-tone), etc., more confusion exists, even though some mutes may be consistent enough *or* some of them may be used extensively *in certain circles*; but only the nucleus mutes are used in all circles *while at the same time* remaining consistent. It may seem surprising to some people for me to recommend the wa-wa here, but even this mute appears in symphonic music as early as Gershwin's *Rhapsody in Blue*.[18] The key word is *consistency*; certainly any active performer will have available other mutes besides this recommended nucleus, depending upon individual needs.

MUTE EFFECTIVENESS

Muting on the trombone generally does not work nearly so well as it does on the trumpet. On the trumpet the bell is closer to the body, and the mutes themselves are smaller, lighter, and cheaper. They are for the most part consistent. Trumpet bells do not vary to such a degree that mute fitting is a problem; therefore, much more variety can be expected from virtually any trumpet player. Conversely, do not expect this same kind of flexibility from the trombonist, as it is just not possible. It is possible to come close, with the exceptional player, but it is not, nor is it ever likely to be, the norm as it is on trumpet. A trumpet player can even entertain the luxurious notion of obtaining a high-quality mute, such as the copper rather than the aluminum wa-wa, whereas the expense would be prohibitive for a trombonist even if quality mutes did exist, which for the most part they do not. For a trombonist to approach the

---

17. A marvelous research project, just waiting for someone, is to find out the mute(s) used on Webern first performances, or performances of his works in which he either conducted or attended. Not only brass players would be enlightened by the results of such a study.

18. This work was actually commissioned by and intended for Paul Whiteman's dance orchestra in 1924 but has since become virtually a standard work in the symphonic repertoire.

flexibility of a trumpet player regarding muting, he or she must have a carefully fitted multitude of costly mutes. Should the trombonist switch instruments, or switch to bass trombone, the entire job must be done over again.

Reasonable flexibility can be achieved with careful practice, and the most important thing is to place mutes where the *left* hand can easily reach them. There will always be occasions when one must remove a mute while still playing.[19] This situation requires careful attention to the position of the instrument: right hand on the slide while maintaining good balance of the instrument. The instrument may be held with the right hand alone in first through fourth positions while sustaining a note and changing mutes. Although these tricks are certainly not encouraged, trombonists should nevertheless know them.

MUTE HARMONICS

One special category of mute sounds remains, and that is what I have termed "mute harmonics." These are of two types. The first is a breakdown of the wa-wa vibrato to u––a––u––a–– done so slowly that different multiphonics emerge depending upon which partial of the harmonic series is present (cf. Chapters I and V).[20] When this is clearly understood, it is possible to "vibrato" the tone between the different partials (the examples recorded give the idea). A similar sound can be produced vocally while subtly altering the mouth cavity and tongue placement. Composers doing so will have a better chance to come to terms with this idea without wasting a lot of performer time, so the practice is heartily recommended for all concerned.

The second of these mute harmonics involves blowing over the top of straight or cup mutes much as one would blow over a beer or soft drink bottle. Some variation is found among mutes (and among blowers), so it is best not to specify definite pitches but to realize that there is a relatively soft fundamental located somewhere in the middle of the staff. There are also two (or more) very loud overtones, the first at about two and one half octaves and the second just a little over three octaves. Both must be used with discretion. This is practical only for trumpet or trombone, the trumpet ones being considerably higher; the horn and tuba mute openings are too large. Of course, each mute must be examined individually, and the reader is encouraged to experiment further regarding *all* aspects of these sometimes baffling and mysterious extensions called mutes.[21]

IXk

---

19. A now classic example of the way it might have been done in the past is seen in bar 107 of the third of the Berg *Three Orchestra Pieces* Op. 6 (1929), Vienna, Universal Edition, 1954, where the second trombonist is directed to "remove third trombonist's mute." He or she must reach over and do this while the third continues playing. There are several examples in the contemporary literature of players removing or inserting mutes while playing.

20. There is a hint of this on the plunger, but it is not very clear; it is a device that is marginal enough on the wa-wa, let alone anything else.

21. For interesting commentary on muting by jazz artists, one is encouraged to read the article "The Talking Trombone in Jazz" by Gerald Sloan, which appears in the *Journal of the International Trombone Association*, Vol. VI (January, 1978), pp. 12-15.

Chapter X:
Means of Extension

There are four methods by which one can extend the trombone into the surrounding environment. Three principal ones will be taken up in this chapter: (1) piano resonance, (2) electronic equipment, and (3) the performance space itself. A fourth way, by water, has already been discussed in Chapter VIII along with other secondary ways, such as resonating gongs, tympani, etc., which are more or less percussive by nature. The garden hose is yet another means of extension, the difference in this case being that the body is extended rather than the trombone. The first of these, piano resonance (along with the garden hose), has always had a special meaning for me, since I have always wanted to move the trombone sound through the performance space without the assistance of electronics. This dream was finally realized in 1972 at the University of Illinois' Krannert Center with the performance of my mixed media ballet *Ten Grand Hosery* ("Ten Grand" refers to pianos, whereas "Hosery" should be obvious). This work has great meaning for this chapter as well as the next on theater (see Appendix II).

PIANO RESONANCE

Xa The fact that each brass instrument is a separate entity can be no more apparent than when working with a piano as a resonator; that is, with the right-hand pedal held in place in a normal manner by the foot or by a pedal block.[1] Each instrument that might be used for blowing into the piano will give a different sound; therefore, the piano ceases to be a piano and becomes an extension of the resonating pipe blown into it. The full range of the trombone works well, though the middle to high range is particularly favorable.

One of the best ways to blow into the piano is to play loud with a diminuendo. The feeling is as though the strings of the piano are crescendoing in their resonance to "take over" the sound from the

---

1. A good pedal block could be a clothespin inserted under the back of the pedal. Other materials might also serve as well; but whatever is used, care should be taken not to jam or force the mechanism. These effects are best on a grand piano, but much can be done with an upright as well. It is imperative that one *experiment* with this. Barney Childs conveyed to me, in 1966, the fascinating bit of information that if one depresses *both* the right-hand pedal *and* the middle (sustaining) pedal, duration and loudness are increased perceptibly. This is important for problems such as the bell rolling in the Krenek *Five Pieces*, which is extremely quiet.

trombone. If done carefully and thoughtfully, one is not sure which instrument is making the sound at any given point; in other words, the technique of "playing in and out of the sound" emanating from the piano is desirable here. It is also interesting to "play in and out of the tuning" or pitch emanating from the piano; that is, it is possible to play one note to set up a resonance and then play the second tone softer but a quarter tone (or some other tone) away from it. Playing the second tone more softly creates equal balance with the sound that is coming out of the piano, and the two can be heard equally. Glissing away slowly, again getting softer from the first established note, will set up very prominent "intonation" beats (see later in this chapter for suggested exercises in this regard).

One fine example of harmonic glissandos on the same note (cf. Chapter III) into the resonating piano appears at the end of the second movement of the Imbrie *Three Sketches.* It adds a whole new dimension to the trombone-piano relationship, bringing about a climactic moment that would otherwise be rather routine. The bridge into the third movement is this resonance, and as it dies away the piano starts the aria. Other works making use of this resonance include Neely Bruce's *Grand Duo*, Robert Suderburg's *Chamber Music III*, and of course Krenek's *Five Pieces*.

As was mentioned before, several percussive devices such as hitting and scraping are possible in a piano. Scraping, rolling, or hitting the bell or mouthpiece are all appropriate sounds from this category (cf. Chapter VIII) because these means create resonances that will "move out into the room." A succession of tones can be played into the piano, and together they can create chords. The performer will do well to experiment a great deal to find out how best to make this resonance work.[2]

ELECTRONICS

The reason for my interest in new sounds was due, in part, to hearing the sounds of electronic music; they acted as a catalyst. During the early sixties, I found that some electronic sounds were repugnant and I wanted to find out why. I concluded that (1) the sounds were unnatural (synthetic) and that (2) I could imitate a great many of them on the trombone. Most important, I felt I could do them a bit better; that is to say, my own trombone imitations of electronic music were less than perfect. I firmly believe that it is the little imperfections that make musical sound, or sound in general, so interesting. Conversely, much electronic sound is too "perfect."

There are notable exceptions, but even these bring home the point. Three works for trombone and tape come to mind: *CHANGES* by Larry Austin, *Animus I* by Jacob Druckman, and Donald Erb's *. . . and then, toward the end. . . .* The first two consist of trombone sound sources woven into a tape which includes synthesized sounds as well. The results are at least good pieces, even if the "perfect" sound factor is there. The Erb piece is totally different in its tape conception, appearing as a "frozen performance" rather than a synthetic tape. As I recorded the source material, the composer performed

---

2. A resonating piano works well with a garden hose, and it can be tucked right in under the piano strings. Garden hoses will be examined further in Chapter XI on theater (see also Appendix II).

at the Moog,[3] choosing registrations as the work progressed. The first "takes" were often "rehearsals," and second and third "takes" had to be made until the proper "performance" was achieved. The result is a piece that theoretically, if not practically, could be performed "live" by five trombonists, four being accompanied by synthesizers — a real electronic chamber piece. It has the spontaneity so lacking in some electronic music, because this work is in part instrumental rather than solely electronic.

Other works using tape, such as Pauline Oliveros's *Theater Piece* or Robert Erickson's *Ricercare á 5*, are simply recorded sound that turned out to be possible "live." Indeed, it was found that the Erickson work was so practical "live" that performances of *Ricercare* are preferred that way. A tape often is really only a substitute for something that might sound better accomplished by another method; this other method might, however, be prohibitively costly or problematical. Usually the audience is served up this sort of acoustical compromise, or a synthetic diet of pure electronics which can be even worse.[4] With these thoughts in mind, consideration of the equipment will be brief. Time does not permit exhaustive discussion, since obsolescence is constantly at hand. The sounds that work best through the equipment are more important for consideration than merely the equipment.

Most players are content with a normal pickup system. Jazz trombonist Urbie Green, however, uses a commonly available mouthpiece pickup to which can be added octave dividers, fuzz tones, and so on; and Swedish jazz artist Eje Thelin uses a mike pickup fastened to the bell[5] (not a contact microphone), which functions like a normal microphone. The advantage of both of these over the normal microphone is that the performer can move around while playing. The mouthpiece pickup requires a hole drilled in the side of the mouthpiece for the pickup to be inserted; an auxiliary mouthpiece is best for this purpose. The advantage is the exclusion of feedback and therefore the comparative ease with which extraneous sound modifications (fuzz, etc.) may be added. The sounds obtained do not seem particularly significant when compared with the "body" sounds that can be amplified, and therefore may not be worth the expenditure. I would recommend waiting for future developments before rushing out to purchase devices;[6] the time will be better spent examining what sounds generally will work best into amplification systems.

---

3. This is the Moog Synthesizer at the Cleveland Institute of Music.

4. These comments do not apply to such people as David Behrman, Gordon Mumma, or David Tudor; their homemade electronic boxes are in and of themselves compositions and require performance. These comments would not apply to Terry Riley either, since his tape delay music is so performance oriented. Similarly, when Loren Rush uses a tape recorder, it becomes an instrument for performance. Pauline Oliveros should be mentioned here also as one who has been known to seek out the imperfections of synthesizers and use these imperfections compositionally. Among a certain segment of electronic artists, at least, the trend is toward more creative circuitry, performance orientation, or both.

5. Made by Caldironi Meazzi, of Milan.

6. Larry Weed, in a letter dated 11 March 1975, states that "today, electromagnetic slides and valves, fibreglass instruments and electronically amplified instruments with readjustable tonal acoustics are the current interest." (Cf. Chapter VII, notes 14 and 15.)

RECOMMENDED SOUNDS FOR AMPLIFICATION

By far the single best category of sounds to amplify are those discussed in Chapter VI (*Other Body Sounds*). Practically everything from that chapter can be used successfully; however, "closed" sounds, esophageal speech, and related material are the areas most open to serious research. These relatively quiet and unusual sounds, when amplified, seem to become new effects rather than just being louder. No doubt this is partly due to the sound emanating through the speaker instead of the trombone and partly due to the fact that the speaker would usually be at a different location than the trombonist. When louder sounds are amplified, one will hear them through the trombone as well as the speaker.

There is, however, something very special about amplified stomach, belching, and retching sounds. Without amplification these sounds seem matter-of-fact; when amplified, they seem to take on a grotesque quality that is very moving indeed, bringing about a dimension I like to think of as "the internal trombone." Because these sounds for the most part are not too loud by themselves, little sound comes from the trombone when they are amplified (see under "Musical Ventriloquism" in Chapter XI). There-

Xb fore, it is very easy to convey a feeling that an electronic tape is being played; that is, the sound can *seem* synthetic, especially if the performer does not make much visual motion at the time. A recorded example demonstrates this clearly; it conveys a "musique concrète" feeling — the altering of non-synthetic sound sources. The sounds certainly will not be accepted as a trombone's, even though these same sounds are all idiomatic — the key word — to the trombone.

Consult the "Amplification and Electronic Effects" chapter (7), written by Arnold Lazarus, in Turetzky's *The Contemporary Contrabass.*[7] Much useful information is contained therein, even though it is designed for a different instrument. The intent of this short section on electronics is to leave the reader with a few notions of what to do with amplification once the electronic hookup has been obtained.

PERFORMANCE SPACE RESONANCE

Performance space is part of the trombone, and, like trombones and players, every space is different. These spaces are extensions of the trombone, just as the trombone is an extension of the body within which the vocal or lip buzzed sound functions. The performer must "play" the space just as much as one would the trombone or body cavity. The trombone has perhaps more control over its acoustical environment than any other instrument because of its dynamic range and directional quality. It is, like the trumpet, an instrument that can be literally "aimed," and this allows for tremendous control of acoustics. Performance space resonance can allow for imaginative thinking in terms of the creative process; it also can cause tremendous problems if this resonance is not clearly understood.

Xc The awareness of resonance is best begun in a room with a long reverberation time. A cathedral will serve this purpose, or a cement stairwell. Whatever the place, first practice chords.[8] Start the

---

7. Bertram Turetzky, *The Contemporary Contrabass* (Los Angeles: University of California Press, 1974), pp. 84-99. This chapter contains an excellent bibliography.

8. Here the term "chords" does not mean "multiphonics" (which are also useful) but rather layers of normal (buzzed) tones.

first note loud and long, and progress by stepped-down dynamics and length to the last note, which is short and soft. An example (1) follows of what might be played:

Example 1: Stepped-down Dynamics and Length in Chord Building

The result should be an echoed sound of all the pitches in equal balance and perfect intonation. The slightest mistake will be heard immediately and will *bother* the player in a way that cannot be duplicated. This chord construction can be done throughout the range, and chords of up to eight, ten, or even more notes can be considered. It is wise to start at the top and work down, as well as the up version noted in the example. Next, try the chord again, but start in the middle range and go in either direction or alternate directions. This is one of the best ways to learn to blow true[9] and to train the ear to listen. Do not get carried away with the beautiful sound quality that this resonance may produce; a resonant room is generally complimentary to the sound. Practice also in "dead" rooms to learn how to work with resonance, to make a "dead" room seem at least slightly resonant. This is not a method of basic *study* material but rather of basic *acoustical* material, if a distinction needs to be made.

The question of using the performance space creatively is an area worthy of development, not unlike the piano resonance where chords can also be set up. Indeed, it is possible to practice the exercises mentioned (see Example 1) into a piano with its pedal down and gain much insight into the technique and into the ear, although a resonant room is actually better. A tape delay system can also be useful for this purpose (cf. note 4 above). One should also play outdoors to study resonance; particularly recommended are canyon and mountain landscapes. There is something very special about playing the trombone outside, and it must be a feeling that didjeridu players take for granted: Resonance is very important to aboriginals even though they are outside (see Appendix III). The trick in using this resonance creatively is to learn to "play into one's own sound,"[10] or to build, construct, play around with, and improvise against the resonance in order to become completely familiar with the trombone and its new environment, while at the same time creating ideas for composition.[11] The key word, again, is *experimentation*. No amount of material in this chapter can substitute for that kind of activity.

---

9. Blowing "true" means blowing with a properly centered tone. The point, in this case, is that one can hear clearly what is wrong if one will listen to the echo carefully.

10. It might be interesting to examine a flute recording, *Paul Horn Inside the Taj Mahal* (1968, Epic Stereo BXN 26466), which gives a taste of what can be done with a 28-second echo. Pay particular attention to the vocal material for its marvelous microtonal fluctuations, keeping in mind the voice-trombone relationship discussed in Chapter II. Also see the more recent recording *Paul Horn Inside the Great Pyramid* (1977, Mushroom Records MRS 5507) for resonance study.

11. An ideal "once-in-a-lifetime" situation presented itself in August, 1976, when I was on a European tour with Merce Cunningham and Dance Company. While I was working with David Behrman and David Tudor at the Pope's Palace in Avignon, a "Great Abbey" (built during the time of Clement

VI in about 1360) was discovered just beyond our performance space, which overlooked the courtyard below where the dancers and the audience were located. With the kind assistance of John Fullemann, sound technician, I not only performed from this "Great Abbey" but I also made several tape recordings in this chapel dealing with its 14-second echo. The trombone sounded beautiful in this space, perhaps due to the irregular surface of the sandstone, and much compositional material was obtained. I have titled these works and sketches *Standing Waves* to reflect the actual acoustic process taking place. Two of these tapes have been recently released on 1750 Arch Records (S-1775) *Stuart Dempster in the Great Abbey of Clement VI*. The compositions have been titled "Standing Waves — 1976" and "Didjeridervish — 1976."

Chapter XI:
Theatrical Implications

Few other instruments can approach the theatrical implications of the trombone: even when it is played normally, the slide moves at least three inches for only a half step. Musical sight-sound relationship is probably nowhere more obvious than in the trombone glissando: everyone knows this visual cliché. When an instrument must extend the throat as well as the arm, the trombone is a much more logical "body extender" than other instruments. It is unique among instruments, and is the only instrument of the body (resonator of body sounds) having a completely variable resonator length. This has implications both acoustically and visually; the latter is dealt with in this final chapter.

GARDEN HOSE

Various references have been made throughout this book to garden hose instruments. As stated before, a garden hose fitted with a trombone mouthpiece is really a trombone of *nonadjustable* length, just as the trombone may be considered an *adjustable*-length garden hose. The first composition[1] that ever considered this idea was Pauline Oliveros's *Theater Piece for Trombone Player and Tape* (note use of the word "player"). No trombone per se is used in this work but rather the acoustical and visual abstractions of it; however, this does not make it any *less* a trombone piece. If this piece were to be for a player of another brass instrument, it would be necessary to use different size hoses and mouthpieces, which would make it an entirely different venture. The hoses are simply resonators and, as such, are no different from any brass of similar length and bore.

These hoses in the Oliveros work were originally "woven" into two sculptures by the choreographer Elizabeth Harris. One, a "candle trumpet," has funnel bells on the end where candles are placed. An extremely tight interrelationship between sight and sound is achieved because the breath of the performer can control the amount and type of light that the candle gives. The other sculpture, a "sprinkler

---

1. Apparently the first composed garden hose solo of extended length was by Robert Hughes, written for me in 1964. It is in his *Anagnorisis*, a ballet for solo dancer, trombone, and percussion (MS), pp. 12-15. This work brought up the interesting problem of wanting to play about nine feet of hose when the dancer needed about fifty feet! Quite a large hole was cut at the nine foot point and a splint arrangement devised, wrapped in matching tape, so that it would not bend and so that anyone observing would think the entire hose was sounding.

horn,"[2] allows for lawn sprinklers to rotate, spewing forth baby powder, smoke, or whatever else might have been loaded in them.[3] Many vocal sounds imitating animals are used (cf. Chapter VI).

My mixed media ballet entitled *Ten Grand Hosery* was inspired largely through my collaboration with Pauline Oliveros and Elizabeth Harris on the *Theater Piece*, and I will always be indebted to them. The sustaining pedals of ten pianos are blocked (cf. Chapter X), the idea being to "send sound through space" from one piano to another. The same score calls for didjeridu (see Appendix III), or an abstraction of it, to be used in the pianos (for the resonance). At one point, the performer is expected to dervish while playing the didjeridu. Also employed is a "sculptorchestra" — that is, sculptured instruments or instrumental sculptures (for a detailed description of this work see Appendix II).

MUSICAL VENTRILOQUISM

The notion that the sound of the instrument always emanates from (or near) the performer is questioned in *Ten Grand Hosery*. Usually, sound comes from the performer, though a notable exception is the pipe organ; the pipes may be some distance from the player. This idea of the sound *leaving* the performer is very easily done with garden hoses, as is seen above, but it is also possible to reverse the process with a trombone in conjunction with a hose and an auxiliary remote player. I remember the Kulturkvartetten (a trombone quartet composed of Folke Rabe, Jan Bark, Runo Ericksson, and Jörgen Johannson) during their performance with me in Copenhagen in 1968. One player on stage held a trombone that played whether he had it to his lips or not. A clear hose hidden from view had been affixed to the "F" attachment slide tube, and the player had only to engage the valve to have the offstage performer's sound come through.[4] The trombone would appear to play by itself — a grand sight indeed![5] (See also under "Recommended Sounds for Amplification" in Chapter X for further information on "musical ventriloquism.")

---

2. This is in no way to be confused with the "trinkler." See Gerard Hoffnung, *The Hoffnung Symphony Orchestra* (London: Dennis Dobson, 1955), p. 38.

3. A very old idea is to blow cigarette smoke through an instrument while playing. Special lighting can make it look as though the instrument is on fire, presumably a "hot tune" being played.

4. I can now appreciate the frustration of the offstage player. Recently (summer, 1975) I had the opportunity to perform on the "didjereunion," a didjeridu-like instrument designed by Phil Carlsen. It is a sculpture instrument made of PVC pipe, and three people can play it at once. The acoustical result is very worthwhile even though the changes that one performer's breathing does to another are absolutely baffling.

5. Harold Betters's Reprise recording (No. 6208) *Out of Sight and Sound* contains notes regarding the recording sessions: ". . . the horn seems on occasion to know what to do without being told. Let us give you an instance: It seems that during the final set of one exhausting late-hours session, a spent and ragged-out Betters neglected to lift his trombone into playing position for the next tune. All the weary Harold could manage to do was pucker up. And lying right there in his lap, that old trombone just took off a-wailin' all by itself."

THEATRICAL CONSCIOUSNESS AND HUMOR

The theatrical trombone probably goes back no further than New Orleans jazz, minstrel shows, and/or vaudeville. It is not a part of New Orleans jazz, really, except that the "tailgaters" of the early 1900s literally had to play over the tailgate of the wagon in order to have room for the slide. Real theatrical consciousness for trombone players probably took hold in the New Orleans era, coming down via vaudeville and the Spike Jones era, directly to contemporary music. One very old idea[6] was to hold the trombone with the bell and slide disconnected, yet close enough to still play; this allowed for the two halves of the instrument to be moved around in all directions. After learning of this, I prepared a small rubber tube that could be stretched over both parts to make a better connection for playing. This allowed the trombone to flop all around and yet still get a good sound. It was even possible to have the bell section crossways in front of the face with the mouthpiece coming in between the braces. Should it accidentally (or purposely) come apart, it might then be desirable to pull the outer slide off, suddenly ending up with many disconnected parts. I often used such shenanigans in shows and other performances during my high school and college days. The idea, apparently, stems from the early nineteen hundreds. Seeing the Spike Jones band in the fifties, there is one sight I will never forget. This was a trombone that had its bell section divided in half so that, apparently, a coupling was constructed in the middle of the curve in the tuning slide. This allowed the bell to drop down *behind* the player and to dangle and swing about. Unfortunately, few early trombonists are famous for humor,[7] although it is known that a few of the great band soloists of that time, such as Leo Zimmerman, liked to play pranks or otherwise engage in humorous activity not related to playing.[8]

LAUGH

The trombone laugh appears throughout the early part of this century.[9] It was often done with the
XIb   wa-wa mute, sometimes coupled with an attempt at the same "ua" vowel sounds by the lip (cf. Chapter

6. This was told to me in the early fifties by my first trombone teacher, the late A. B. "Chic" Moore.

7. Glenn Bridges, in a letter dated 27 August 1974 (small changes have been made for the sake of brevity and clarity): "Jim Miller was a Holton demonstrator back in the twenties and before. He used to do a stunt like faking a bagpipe in the lower register — and good. That fellow really had a fantastic range. . . . The trombone laugh was probably originally done by Fred Innes back in the 1880s, for private audiences, not in concert. Although a concert artist, Innes did all of the so-called stunts. The first laugh I ever heard on a record was Harry Raderman's *Make That Trombone Laugh* on an old Edison disc made in 1920. Yes, I heard the stunt of dismantling the trombone and playing through the upper tuning slide only. I remember a Larry Conley doing this in an orchestra pit in 1923 playing *When Hearts Are Young* with Rodemich's Orchestra in St. Louis. Many did these things even before, [and] I heard all kinds of trombone stunts as far back as I can remember. I began . . . on trombone in 1911, [and] vaudeville artists were then in the "swing" as they say today. Fellows like Eddie Coe, etc., etc."

8. Glenn Bridges, *Pioneers in Brass* (Detroit: Sherwood Publications, 1965), p. 111 (book available from the author, 15626 Callahan, Fraser, Michigan 48026).

9. Cf. note 7 above.

II) to reinforce the effect.[10]   An extended example appears in Robert Suderburg's *Chamber Music III*[11] in the "Brother Devil" (third) movement. Here the trombonist uses the wa-wa while the pianist makes vocal "Ha-ha" sounds in imitative counterpoint. Other kinds of laughing are heard when a trombonist attempts to play such famous tunes as "Hora Staccato" or "Flight of the Bumblebee" while a crowd (or the band) laughs at the performer.[12]   For some reason, the trombone seems to take to this kind of comedy more than the other brass instruments, perhaps because of the apparently awkward slide work that most people assume mirrors the trombonist. Whatever the reasons, they are cause for many people not to take the instrument seriously — as seriously as the cello or piano, for instance.

THEATER PIECES

Other than the type of incidental theater that occurs in Cage's *Solo*, the first real theater piece for trombone solo to achieve international fame was the Berio *Sequenza V*. Of course, *all* music is theatrical; that is, the performance of any piece is of interest visually as well as acoustically. The Berio is one of two works to arrive on the music scene simultaneously, each with a distinct flavor of its own in this genre of music theater. The Oliveros *Theater Piece* and the Berio work were programed on my premiere concerts of 21 and 22 March 1966 at the San Francisco Tape Music Center. No doubt there are other earlier theater pieces, but none, so far as is known, received such a wide distribution.[13]

Perhaps the Erickson *Ricercare á 5* should be included as a music theater piece, but the only actions observed are those necessary to perform the work. As in the Cage piece, it is impossible to make the trombone *not* theatrical. These Cage and Erickson works are what might be termed "implied theater"; that is, they seem to be theater pieces in all respects except that nothing has been added to the movements necessary to execute the work acoustically. Granted, the Cage work could have a specific theatrical option exercised by a performer, but this option need not be taken.

PERSONALITY PORTRAYAL

The Berio *Sequenza V*, being the first real solo theater piece for trombone, does warrant some discussion. It is a "story" about the famous European clown Grock,[14] and the trombonist's actions acoustically

---

10. I remember the "Blondie and Dagwood" radio shows during the forties and fifties when about once a month or so the following remark, imitated by a wa-wa muted trombone, came from Mr. Dithers, Dagwood's boss. He would say: "Bumstead!! (*Ua*-ua-) Come into my office!! (uauauaua*Ua*-ua)." Currently, the role of the schoolteacher in the "Charlie Brown" cartoons on television is played by a wa-wa muted trombone.

11. See pages 19-21 of the score.

12. A classic is Tommy Pederson's solo on "The Jones Laughing Record" recorded by the Spike Jones Band on RCA LSC-3235(e).

13. *Bolos* by Rabe and Bark is apparently the first theater piece (1962), but this is for four trombones.

14. Stage name for Charles Adrien Wettach, born in Switzerland in 1880, died in Italy in 1959. His most famous acoustical trademark was his speaking of the word "why." Berio often told me I was like Grock, which may explain the "why" of the piece.

and visually attempt to portray this story. In the beginning, the player "shoots" something in the air (ducks?), which may appear to be high or low. This becomes faster, more frequent, and more disjointed, until finally the whole situation becomes so frantic and hysterical that the performer can only utter a bewildered "Why?" (at the end of line 3 of the score). From that point on, the player must breathe in while playing (cf. Chapter VI), interject loud notes into a soft texture, work the slide vigorously, and otherwise maintain a level of hysteria that represents Grock and how he might have performed had he been a trombone player. The hysteria conveyed is not falsely imposed; it is also the result of performing the piece! One need not *try* to be theatrical except at the beginning and at the spoken word. On the other hand, the player constantly must have in mind the message that is to be conveyed, and to keep that level up. The hallmark of the true clown is the mixture of the comic and tragic, and this must be kept in mind. Special lighting sets the mood for the piece.

Stretching role-playing further, I, in one sense, never appeared at all in my *Life Begins at Forty* concert.[15] T. Peter Tomita's review may partially explain why:

> One creepy green spotlight dimly focused on stage left. Enter the Carnivore of Uranus exploring "an alien environment accompanied by vague sensations of an almost forgotten previous existence wherein he was frolicked in the canals 'neath sunny skies in search of Corvo" (from program notes by the composer). It's Stuart Dempster! Costumed in green tights, green rubber feet and hands, a massive headpiece covered with green and clear cellulose dangling, obscuring what look to be ordinary motorcycle goggles on what should be his head (but not *quite* sure). He (It) is scooting about the floor on a small caster. The trombone, also dressed in green and clear cellulose, is playing the *Carnival of Venice* in harmony with the electronic tape. The carnivore stops to contemplate, then scoots in and around the audience when we realize more sounds are emanating from this being than trombone. Yes! The Carnivore is wired with half a dozen speakers connected to the tape.
>
> *Hi-Lites from the Carnivore of Uranus for Trombone and Tape* by Edwin London was the opening number of a concert . . . [which] also included *Bombardments No. 4* by Robert Moran in which Dempster futilely fights his way out of a gigantic burlap bag, *Whatzit No. 6* by Raymond Wilding-White in which he performs through a cardboard refrigerator packing crate, and his now famous *General Speech* by Robert Erickson. . . .[16]

In all these works I never appeared as a "trombonist" but rather as an outer-space being, a larva, a speech giver, and a mechanized robot. In Wilding-White's *Whatzit No. 6* (1970), I pop up and down like a jack-in-the-box, quoting, like spliced tape, many excerpts from the trombone literature. One should also be aware of Wilding-White's *Encores for Stu* (1970), fourteen little pieces suitable for the end of a concert, which involve every imaginable activity that one might do with a trombone. My favorites include "Nocturne" (No. 10) where bubbles are blown through the "F" attachment, and "Aerodynamics" (No. 11) where a balloon is installed on the "F" attachment so that when the trigger is engaged the balloon blows up. Pedagogical problems abound when one begins to learn Robert Moran's *Bombardments No. 4* (1964 and 1968), an incredible piece because it must be performed in a large burlap bag.[17] I eventually learned to fall, roll, and tumble while still playing the trombone, but not before practicing

---

15. This concert was in Seattle at the *and/or* on 8 July 1976.

16. "Stu Dempster at and/or," in *Ear*, Vol. 4, No. 7, Fall 1976.

17. This "costume" was designed by Renko Ishida and the composer.

more elementary procedures. This practice entailed (1) learning to fall *without* the trombone while *in* the bag, (2) learning to fall *with* the trombone while *not* in the bag, and (3) learning to play the piece. I then combined the first two procedures, finally adding the last one. The result is a writhing "blob" with seemingly many legs — the trombone contributes its share — and the trombone (and the trombonist) seem to be a larva in a cocoon during the pupa stage. The *Bombardments* is a trombonist's "Rite of Spring."

Some of the best theater in music is that which is linked to a high degree with the sound, as in the Berio or the Oliveros. The candles in the Oliveros work are affected by the blowing or by the twirling of the hose producing the Doppler effect in the sound, the latter relating in some strange way to dervishing with the didjeridu. This spinning is done just as well with the trombone. Also, with the Ben Johnston *One Man*, discussed in Chapters IV and VIII, the gestures undertaken are simply those which also best execute the sound desired, even though the work seems to be a theater piece. In Johnston's work, the wind chimes over the face are theatrical, to be sure, but do create a wonderful sound. The rolling up of the pants legs to reveal the finger cymbals is certainly theatrical but nonetheless necessary in the acoustical performance of the work.[18] Notice the difference in Robert Erickson's *General Speech* where "hard stares," actions with a glass of water, and so on form only a small part of the total theatrical picture (see Appendix I).

The great success of *General Speech* is due, no doubt, to its careful extension of the trombone bell as the throat, and the slide as the arm. It is a parody of a real speech with as many theatrical gestures as practical to portray the person behind this speech. In this way it is not unlike *Sequenza V*, a story about a specific individual, the main meaning being behind his public image. Although the actions are designed to portray the person at hand as General MacArthur,[19] it is freely recognized that the person could be anyone. It is not *what* is being said, it is *how*!

One might well imagine an opera being carried on by several trombones.[20] Indeed, understanding of many opera plots would not be any the less enhanced. Only when opera is composed with *all* the parts created for trombones instead of voices, with great trombone opera choruses "vocalizing" the refrains, can the trombone truly be said to have arrived at the foyer of mainstream western music.

---

18. A word about dress: When such actions are done in, say, full dress (tails), the impact is altogether different than if one is in jeans or even a dark suit. The strict formality of the concert setup as represented by the formal clothes is more apparent when the deviations of pant leg rolling, wearing short pants, etc., are made. This juxtapositioning of various symbols of the traditional and the new is very important and should be constantly in mind when performing new works requiring theater.

19. Perhaps the trombone is the ultimate corncob pipe.

20. The original trombone opera plot came to my mind in the fall of 1973 upon returning from Australia. The "Watergate Hearings" on the infamous Watergate Hotel Break-In, 17 June 1972, had begun several months earlier and were occupying television time morning, noon, and night. The voices droned on, and the participants seemed to speak slowly and otherwise appear listless. Being gone for four months, and returning to hear the same Hearings grinding away, it was as though time had stopped. At this point the realization came that, by extending the *General Speech* idea, the entire Watergate Affair is one of the world's great (1) drone pieces, (2) theater pieces, and (3) potential trombone pieces.

Backword

The trombone is a symbol of long life. It is the instrument which remains unchanged, just as it is an instrument only rarely used until the twentieth century. For five hundred years it has continued with only small changes, while the rest of western instruments have undergone drastic changes or have been invented.

The trombone, then, is a sleeping giant just beginning to awaken. This book of elementary ideas can provide only the material for the giant's first breakfast. Readers must realize that this book is in the form of a first word — a foundation — upon which much can be built.

This cannot be a book of combined elements, and although various hints toward combining elements have been made from time to time, they are given with the idea of helping the trombonist or composer to experiment further. To spend any real time on "element combining" would take several volumes, be too pedantic, and stifle the reader's (and my own) imagination. If the reader has read this far, it is time for him or her to *experiment* (and this will be true whether reading from the back of the book or from the front).

Those readers who have begun at this end of the book will have already discovered the recording. The discs are organized with examples from throughout the book. In reading from this end, one will be going from the outside in; that is, from the theatrical gesture, to performance space, through the trombone, and into the body. Even the miscellanea chapter turns out to be in the middle.

When the appendices are read first, they will lend a background perspective to the book that can be helpful. On the other hand, in reading from the front, the reader will find the appendices useful in the order they are mentioned in the chapters (see Foreword). From the front, the reader starts with the body and works through the trombone and out into the space surrounding. There is really no difference whether one is in or out of the body, neither being better than the other. It is all the same, the end being the beginning and the beginning being the end. Welcome or farewell, then, depending upon the route traveled!

Appendix I:
General Speech

General Speech by Robert Erickson is one of the most amazing and thought-provoking works ever composed for the trombone. This work is reproduced in its entirety on the following pages because of its importance for study and its relationship to this book.

The text is from General Douglas MacArthur's retirement speech given at West Point.[1] One should consult MacArthur's own autobiography[2] for pictures, speech texts, and other information helpful to the prospective performer.

Setup

The setup should include the most opulent lectern one can muster. On it should be situated a blacklite, and two red lights on a dimmer, placed so as to light the medals and the hat. Two smallish American flags should grace the highest point of the lectern thus: ⊥⊤. To the right side of the lectern, or better yet, on an auxiliary table, a glass and a pitcher of water should be placed. Behind the lectern a series of steps varying in two-inch heights should be placed out of audience view. The dimmer for the red lights should be conveniently placed on the lectern so it can be used when standing at full height, whereas the blacklite switch should be located near the floor (or series of steps) to be operated while bent down (see lighting cue sheet).

Performance

Walk on brusquely in a military fashion and mount next to highest step with bent knees so as to appear standing on the floor. The trombone should then be brought up suddenly followed by a hard stare

---

1. Listen to the MGM recording E 4245 General of the Army Douglas MacArthur - the Life and Legend of the Old Soldier - a documentary compiled from Hearst Metrotone Newsreels.

2. MacArthur, Douglas, Reminiscenes (McGraw-Hill, New York, 1964).

General Speech

a composition by

Robert Erickson

for

Trombone Solo (1969)

Commissioned, Edited, and Annotated by

Stuart Dempster

Costume and Lighting by Lenore Erik-Alt

Dress

The performer is to wear full dress (tails) to simulate a full dress military uniform. On the coat should be worn medals and other insignia as appropriate. An abstraction of a military hat should be properly decorated, and all insignia, medals, or decorations should be painted with "da-glo" (fluorescent) paint. Dark glasses, shoulder pads, and white satin gloves will complete the costume (a corncob pipe, although appropriate to the personage represented, should not be used).

and pointed jaw. After the first statement, unbend the knees by raising to full height suddenly (everything about this work should appear just a bit too large, too high, too long, etc.).

As best as possible, one is to perform the vowels and consonants as seen in the word abstractions in the large lettering (the speech is given only as an aid). This means shaping the mouth, tongue, and throat in all different manners in order to achieve the desired effect, and it will no doubt be found that a comprehensive analysis of each sound will have to be made.

This piece requires an "F" attachment trombone. It will be noticed, however, that the only use of the valve made is for the half valve effect. Where there is call for pitches below the low E they are designated as "fake" meaning "fake trigger" notes; that is, they should be performed as bent tones or as what Robin Gregory in his book on The Trombone[3] refers to as "priveleged" notes. Do not engage the trigger for any low note except at the very end of line 19 about where the word "Pedal F" is written. The "etc." at that point should be morebent trigger pedals down to as low as possible.

All vibratos can be assumed to be the "diaphragm" (or "gut") vibrato with occasionally a small hint of a jaw vibrato when appropriate.

Pauses

The first long pause in the middle of line 6 should be taken very matter-of-factly. Stick out the chest to show off the medals. Bring

instrument back up abruptly.

The second long pause at the end of line 16 must be carefully timed so that all the little niceties can be accomplished in the allotted time. Earlier (in line 16) there is an "ahem" which must be carefully sealed into the mouthpiece so that it all comes through the trombone. Do it vocally as though it were really necessary. The "cough" later on should be a surprise; yet care must be taken to seal carefully the lips on the mouthpiece so that it goes through the instrument. At the double bar - "Ahem (Belch)" - throw hand over bell (as a lecturer would do covering the mouth). It should be very hurried - the drink of water is urgent! - for the first ten or twelve seconds. Then slow down the pace gradually moving into the body quiver at the beginning of line 17, the body quiver being of an old man regaining his composure.

Surprise Ending

At the end of the piece bring instrument down suddenly (taking care to allow medals to show). After stage (and house) lights are blacked count two seconds and dim red lights off. In just the blacklite slowly "fade away" as gradually and slowly as possible behind the podium by bending the knees, etc. When completed, turn off blacklite, move away from lectern into a bow, and stay there until house lights come on. Then walk on and off in military fashion until bows are complete. If a third or fourth bow is called for, a wave of the hat is desirable, but maintain the character of the personage right through the final exit.

3. Praeger, New York, 1973.

Lighting Cue Sheet

The piece is performed in its entirety in normal stage lighting. It is at the end of the piece itself that this changes. In order to know when the end comes one only need know that the trombone is brought down three (3) times, the third time being the end.

When the instrument is brought down:
(a) the first time, about 1/3 into the piece, a water glass is used.
(b) the second time, about 2/3 into the piece, a water glass and pitcher are used.
(c) the third time marks THE END of the piece and the

Lighting person will:

**count 2 seconds after end of piece and black the stage and house lights suddenly (do not dim).

The performer will then count 2 seconds and dim red lights, remaining in blacklite. While disappearing behind podium performer will turn off blacklite (the performer must be aware that the blacklite will appear off to the lighting person once performer has disappeared out of blacklite, even if it is not yet switched off!)

**count 8 seconds after blacklite goes off and bring up stage and house lights suddenly. (Applause will then start and piece is over.)

For performer on stage:
Prepare 2 red lights dimmed low facing up from podium on chest and head, etc.
Prepare blacklite on podium to pick up medals, etc.
Both systems remain on during entire playing of the piece, then;
Follow performer directions above.

84

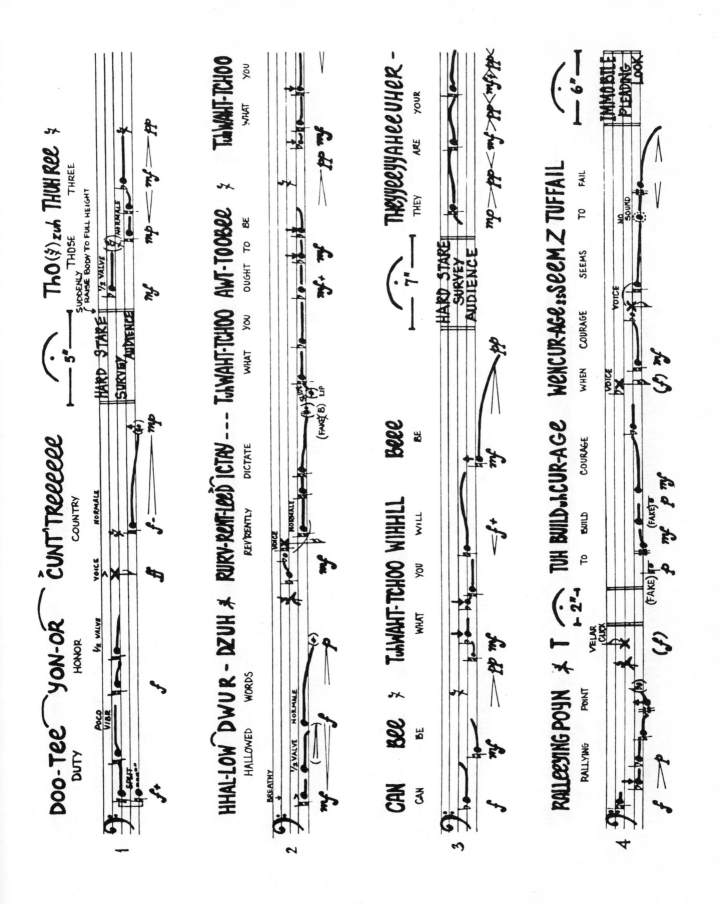

85

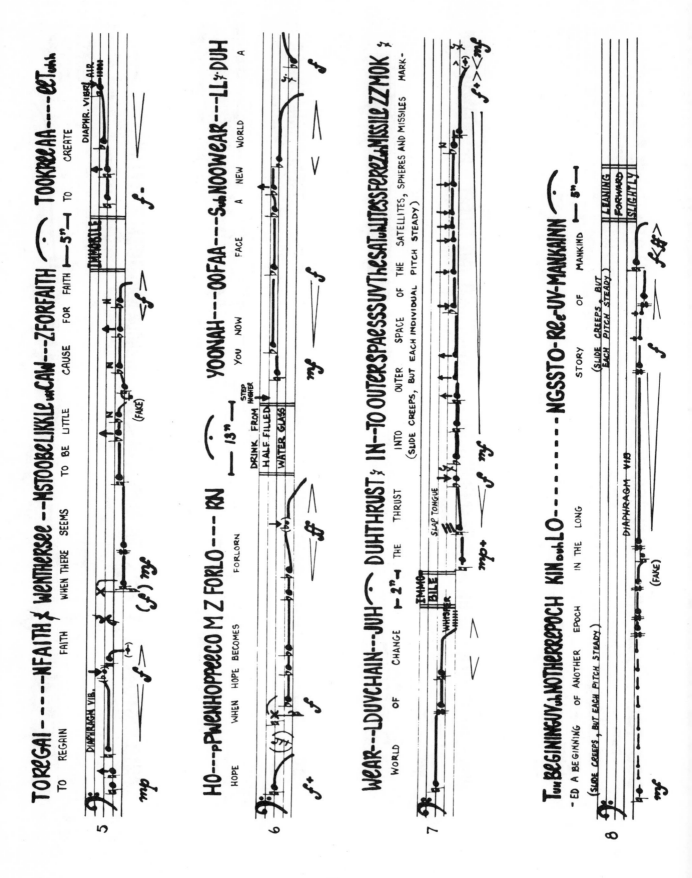

86

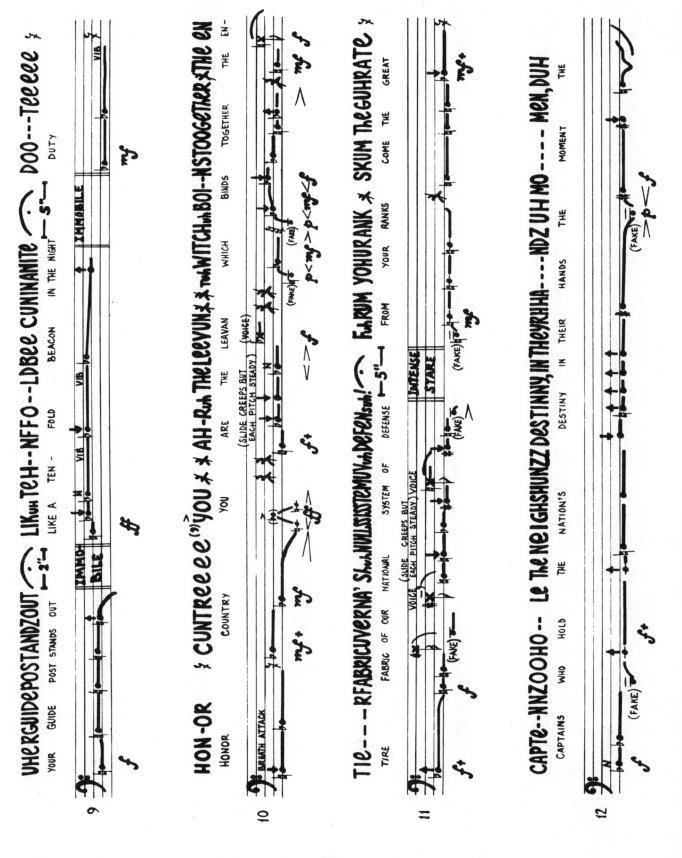

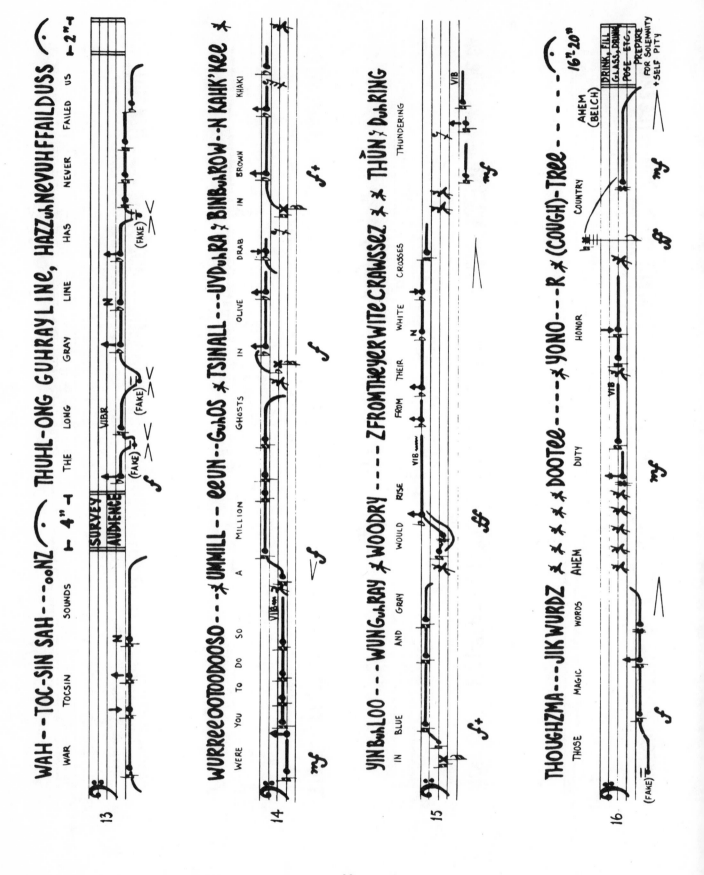

88

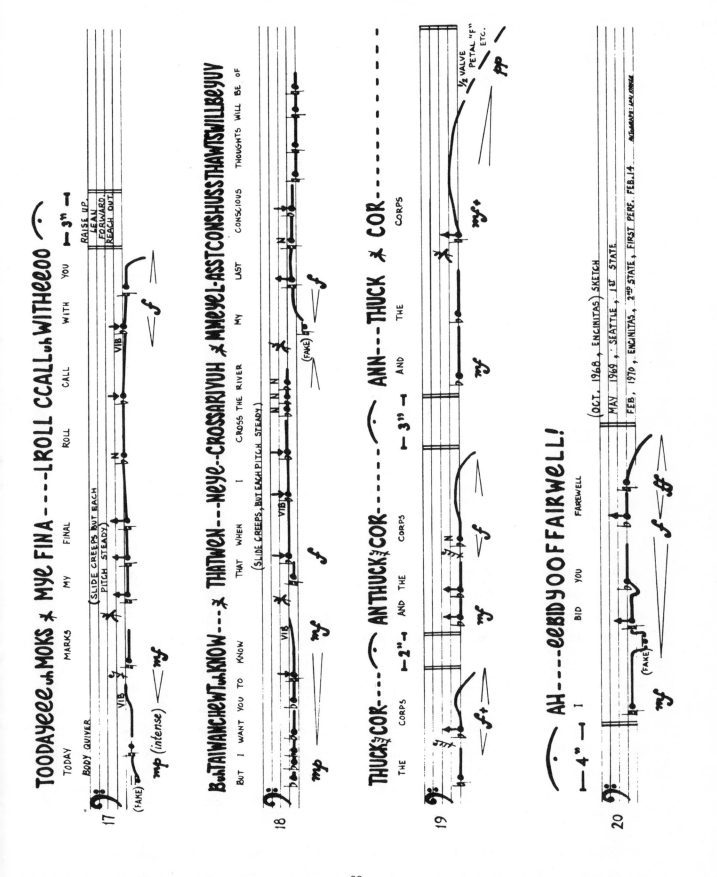

89

Appendix II:
Ten Grand Hosery

a composition by
STUART DEMPSTER
for Musician, Dancer, Sculptorchestra, Supplementary Dancers, and Audience
Composed with the assistance of Al Huang
and Dedicated to Pauline Oliveros

Premiered February 9th and 10th, 1972
Festival Theater — Krannert Center, University of Illinois, Urbana
Stuart Dempster, assisted by Al Huang and his Tai Chi classes, and by graduate sculpture students of Frank Gallo. Lighting by Ray Caton. Production by Gordon Smith. Title contributed by Ben Johnston. Sculptures: *Blowdozer* by Wayne Forbes, *Human Serpentoid* by Chip Wulff, *Potballers VII and IX* and *Lift to Top and Let Drop* by Mike Hoeft.

STAGE

The stage should be as open as possible, with all curtains including the cyclorama raised up out of sight. Place ten grand pianos on the stage with the lids raised and sustaining pedals blocked so that the strings will be free to resonate. Arrangement should be casual, yet spread around the stage to cover the area generally with a semicircle leaving the downstage center open. Ten garden hoses with as many trombone mouthpieces should be stretched, one from each piano, to the center of the stage, the ends of the hoses being hooked in the sounding board holes so that they will not slip out. All hoses should be of a length so that the musician can stand up and have all hoses rise evenly. Each hall encountered will, of necessity, require small changes in the conception, including the number of pianos used. The title remains the same no matter how many pianos are used. It is never to be done with less than three pianos, and all that are used should be grands.

LIGHTING

Lighting should be simple even if many lights are hung for the occasion. Concentration should be on washes of blue and gold, these being the best choices with green or clear plastic garden hoses. Specials can be hung for downstage center, stage center, and as desired elsewhere. No specific lighting is necessary for any of the following numbers other than a general increase from no light to a lot of light, and then back to nothing again. An element of improvisation is desired for all elements in this piece, including the lighting.

PERFORMANCE

I. *Grand Overture and Didjeridervish*
Musician will come out on stage with a didjeridu or, preferably, an abstraction of it such as a PVC sewer pipe of about one and a half inches in diameter and about three and a half to four feet long. Move slowly at first to each piano, making soft sounds most of which are vocal. Gradually add occasional buzzed sounds as the sound works up a bit louder and busier. Go round and round to all the pianos moving quietly here, staying and blowing longer there, as much as practical having didjeridu (or sewer pipe) pointed into piano to pick up resonance. It should seem as though you are "testing" pianos and that the piece has not really begun yet. Gradually move to each piano faster, going around faster until finally working way to center down stage in a full dervish at the rate of one rotation for every two seconds. By this time continuous droning by the method of circular breathing should be going on which will, by the way, create a Doppler effect of microtones because of the rotating. Keep this up three to eight minutes, then gradually slow down and finally stop, sink to knees slowly and bring didjeridu up overhead while going down on back in a yoga "fish" or "diamond" asana with back off the floor and top of head touching floor in such a way that the didjeridu reaches floor and can still be played. Continue circular breathing gradually getting softer and fading out.

Dancer starts far upstage just moving casually with perhaps a few traditional type warmups or whatever else seems appropriate. Work way finally to pianos, neither avoiding nor seeking out musician. An occasional shout or grunt into a piano is appropriate, thereby making dancer a musician just as musician becomes dancer. Include occasional spins and/or short three to four second dervishes. As musician finally reaches center stage and dervishes, make no more sounds but concentrate on dancing round and round the musician, sometimes the same speed or faster or slower. Change directions frequently, or whatever seems appropriate. Through all this remember to be meditative, comfortable, relaxed, and happy! Gradually end up lying on the stage at about the same time or just after the musician lies on the stage. When sound stops, lie motionless.

II. *Ten Grand Hosery — Part One*
Musician, while stage is blacked, moves to center stage where the "bouquet of mouthpieces" is, and sits crosslegged with mouthpieces to his mouth. As lights come up, gradually make a few vocal sounds, then a few buzzed sounds, into the favorite garden hose-piano instruments that are at hand. Gradually work up to using all hoses, the idea being to "send" sound from one piano to the other. Lots of long tones, vibrato (microtonal wavers), bending notes, etc., are appropriate so that microtonal chord structures are set up in the piano strings. It is also not a bad idea to have an eleventh hose going to "nowhere" so that the dancer can occasionally play (on the far end). Stand up once, at a dramatic

moment, so the hoses can all rise together. Bang mouthpieces together occasionally. Musician will want to "dance" occasionally just as dancer will want to make sound, and this must be carefully worked out between the two. Gradually fade out to silence and lie on back. Total time: 8-15 minutes.

Dancer will begin at the spot where the last piece was ended. Gradually make some activity as appropriate, but give musician a head start. Dancer will eventually want to dance "through" hoses, etc., and contribute a few sounds from time to time. A hose can be brought loose from a piano, musician can move, and movements with hose, dancer, and musician can be improvised as desired. Dancer will no doubt want to dance with and become entangled in one or more hoses. Banging hoses on floor is useful, just as musician will bang mouthpieces occasionally, but this should not be excessive. (Option: If more than one dancer is used for this section — combining Parts I and II — the solo dancer should still begin first, perhaps for four or five minutes, before bringing in the supplementary dancers lying on stage amongst the pianos.) Gradually slow down motions, ending up silent and motionless as sound stops and lights fade.

III. *Divertimento for Sculptorchestra*
Various sculpture instruments may be used. These may be instruments that have been made especially interesting to view, or else sculptures that have the ability to make sound or that can be played. No restrictions are imposed other than that they ought to be (but do not necessarily have to be) of tubes, or tubular. In the first performance, for instance, tubes with little balls running through them were used, the balls dropping into various containers and on drums, etc. Some were buzzed lip "instruments" with trombone mouthpieces. It is assumed that successive performances will see a larger sculptorchestra of new instruments plus some of those constructed for previous performances that will, one day, be of a number and variety to be an entire "piece" or program in and of themselves. It is a nice touch if the sculpture artists themselves play their own instruments; however, this is not necessary.

IV. *Grand Grand Fanfare and Ten Grand Hosery — Part Two*
The fanfare is played using a short garden hose instrument played into the sewer pipe for resonance. An announcement is made, either by musician or dancer, that the audience is invited to lie on the floor amongst the pianos. A repeat of II then takes place, but musician concentrates mainly on washing the audience with sound. After a period of time, dancer can rise slowly and eventually invite audience to dance too. It is nice if eight or ten other dancers can be brought in first by the dancer, and then have them assist in leading the audience.

V. *Grand Grand Grand Finale*
Continue as in IV, but have pianos moved back off stage out of the way. Sculpture instruments can rejoin, especially if any are sturdy enough to be handled and played by the audience. Have dancing dissolve into a social get-together in such a way as to cloud just when the piece ends. All this is enhanced if wine and/or coffee can be served with things to eat. To move outside to a grand festival of some sort, with picnic or barbecue, would be an ideal finale. A sculptorchestra street parade would not be inappropriate.

Appendix III:
The Didjeridu

Anyone casually aware of the fact that the only musical instrument (apart from the ubiquitous bullroarer and simple percussive devices such as sticks, boomerangs and, rarely, a hollow log drum) used by the Aborigines is the *didjeridu* may well wonder what there is to study, instrumentally speaking, in Australian Aboriginal music. On listening carefully to a large amount of didjeridu music, however, one becomes aware of two things: first, that there is extraordinary variety and ingenuity behind the apparent monotony of its drone, and, second, that a remarkable virtuosity of technique is displayed by expert players of the instrument. Although a fairly full appreciation of the former can be achieved by concentrated listening, transcription into musical notation, and painstaking analysis, the latter can be thoroughly understood only by attempting to master the instrument oneself in as authentic a manner as possible.

This statement opens the paper entitled "The Didjeridu" by Trevor A. Jones in *Studies in Music*, Vol. 1.[1] A. P. Elkin provides further comment in his book *The Australian Aborigines*:[2]

The most interesting Aboriginal musical instrument is the didjeridu, but it is only known in Eastern Kimberley and the northern third of the Northern Territory. It is an un-stopped hollow piece of bamboo or wood, usually the latter, about four or five feet long, and two inches or even more in internal diameter, with a mouth-piece made of wax or hardened gum. The player blows into the instrument in trumpet fashion. The precision and variety of rhythm produced on the didjeridu are very striking. Sometimes it sounds like a deep bourdon organ stop being played continuously; at other times like a drum beaten in three-four time, and so on, varying according to the type of song and dance which it is accompanying, and indeed, "carrying." The tongue lies flat, with the lip at times projecting into the mouthpiece. The continuous nature of the sound is most remarkable. The diaphragm rises as breath is taken, and the next over a second later, but some of the incoming air is kept in the mouth to be blown into the instrument while a quick intake is being made. Glass-blowers may understand.

The technique of playing the didjeridu is, indeed, incredible. One must begin with the relatively simple "circular" or "continuous" breathing, a technique which most brass players find difficult. On top of this are the use of the voice humming the tenth (or some other interval) above the fundamental

---

1. Perth: University of Western Australia Press, 1967, pp. 23-55.
2. Sydney: Angus and Robertson, 1964, 4th ed., pp. 247-248.

to make double stops, the use of the tongue injected in the tube, the use of the first overtone either "hooted" like a steamboat whistle or "spat" like a gunshot, the use of the voice scream in a kind of coyote yell (dingo howl), and the use of vowel sounds which are made by the alteration of the mouth and throat cavity. All of these, including the circular breathing, can be used separately or in various combinations to create rhythm patterns, many of which are tremendously complex. Although the drone of the continuous sound dulls the senses of the listener (and, incidentally, that of the player as well), it is the complexity of the rhythmic factors that heightens the awareness. The very intricate minute changes suddenly become very great, and the large variations become overwhelmingly powerful. The aboriginals often play into a tin can, bucket, or other handy item for more resonance, one player even using an outboard motor cover![3]

No other lip reed seems to be in such a high state of development, western brass instruments included. I am indebted to Robert Erickson, for it was he who first introduced the instrument to me in 1967. My interest in the didjeridu came about as a result of our working on the *Ricercare á 5* together. The didjeridu then became part of the inspiration of *General Speech*. In any case, the instrument has been a constant source of inspiration ever since, due to so much of the didjeridu technique having direct application to the trombone.

Didjeridu mouthsounds are the key to learning didjeridu playing, and this is not unlike the western brass player's use of "tu" and "ku" to describe double tonguing. However, with the didjeridu, it is virtually a "way" of mastering the instrument. Young children, around the age of six or seven, will be instructed in mouthsounds without even using an instrument (they will have been blowing on a didjeridu since they were perhaps three or four), so that when they go back to blowing on the instrument they will have all the elements in their head. It is not unlike what I so often do in my teaching by having students buzz without the trombone (or mouthpiece) to gain embouchure awareness and to train the ear; however, for the most part, trombone playing and buzzing are two quite separate experiences, whereas didjeridu playing and mouthsounds (which sometimes include buzzing) may actually be the same. The enunciation of the vowel sounds while playing the didjeridu is extremely important; the sounds must have a clarity resembling speech. Properly studied mouthsounds accomplish this admirably.[4]

I am interested in this relationship between the didjeridu and the trombone both for the interesting new sounds that can be derived and the teaching methods used. Fortunately, I was able to make a visit to Australia and engage in some fieldwork in the Northern Territory, where most of the didjeridu playing takes place. This visit was during August 1973, carried out with a Fulbright-Hays Award under the auspices of the Australian-American Educational Foundation with assistance from the Australian

---

3. I observed this in Numbulwar, Northern Territory, during August 1973.

4. The reader is encouraged to study *Songs from the Northern Territory* (1964), particularly record number two (there are five 12-inch discs and one handbook). These are available from the Australian Institute of Aboriginal Studies, P.O. Box 553, Canberra City, A. C. T. 2601, or Humanities Press Inc., 171 First Avenue, Atlantic Highlands, New Jersey 07716. This record collection is by Alice M. Moyle. One should also be on the lookout for Moyle's *Aboriginal Sound Instruments*, a book and a record soon to be released by the Australian Institute of Aboriginal Studies.

Institute of Aboriginal Studies. I am deeply grateful to these organizations for making this study possible. It is hoped that I can return soon to continue this research, for it is felt that the aboriginal people have a great deal to teach the western world about wind playing in general and lip reeds in particular. The trombone may seem old when compared to western orchestral instruments, but it is only a five-hundred-year-old baby when compared to the possible two- to four-thousand-year-old tradition of the didjeridu. The time has come to examine the didjeridu in depth, for the aboriginals hold answers to questions that trombonists and other brass players are just beginning to learn how to ask.

Appendix IV:
John Cage and Frank Rehak

The *Solo for Sliding Trombone* by John Cage has become a classic in its own time. The *Solo* may be the first truly avant garde piece for trombone; certainly it is the first piece for trombone of an avant garde nature to receive any sort of fame. The *Solo* is actually pages 173-184 of the orchestral parts of the *Concert for Piano and Orchestra* (1957-58),[1] and the first paragraph of the relatively copious instructions tell a great deal about the work:

> The following 12 pages for a trombone player may be played with or without other parts for other players. It is therefore a trombone solo or a part in an ensemble, symphony, or concerto for piano with orchestra. Though there are 12 pages, any amount of them may be played (including none).

The piece demands much from the performer. The performer may take the role of composer or improvisor as well as the role of music reader; silence must also be dealt with. These choices must be made, and then within that more choices will be necessary. The most amazing aspect about the *Solo* is its uncanny ability to always be a John Cage work and not the work of someone else. It should go without saying that the *Solo* is one of the most important trombone works of our time, and should be acquired for careful study.

My own personal approach to this piece is not unlike a jazz player's treatment of a "lead sheet" (a lead sheet is simply a melody with the chord symbols). A jazz player takes a "lead sheet" or "tune" and builds either simple elaborations or perhaps an entire twenty- or thirty-minute piece. The Cage *Solo* is similar; one can choose to make it simple or elaborate, and in my approach I tend to make a rather involved philosophical statement coupled with lighthearted buoyancy. To me the *Solo* is a meditation with particular attention to breathing patterns and theatrical considerations. It is a constant source of food for thought, and every time I work with the piece it seems to say something new. It is this factor that makes the *Solo* one of the most difficult works I have ever performed. When one realizes that I recommend about 200 hours of practice for Ben Johnston's *One Man* or that I have spent about 300 hours on *General Speech* by Robert Erickson, one might be able to appreciate the kind of demands the Cage *Solo* makes — or *can* make. Here again, this may be a choice of the performer; one does not have to opt for a big production, but in my own view it is necessary.

---

1. New York: Henmar Press, sole distributors C. F. Peters, 1960.

Because of the jazz lead sheet idea, I was, of course, most interested when Cage told me that the piece had been written for Frank Rehak. Rehak distinguished himself as a fine jazz trombonist playing with many of the great bands of the '40s, '50s, and '60s. He also had a background of classical training as a cellist and pianist, and this combination of classical and jazz background made him an ideal person for Cage to work with. Cage felt that Frank's special talents were what made the trombone part such a good one. The story of Frank Rehak is capsulized in an interview in *down beat*,[2] where Frank explains, among other things, his teaching at Synanon Foundation, which has now become his whole life. I contacted Frank to find out what he could tell me about John Cage and his *Solo*, and I sent him a copy of the score. Here follows a beautiful account of the story of this work, in Frank Rehak's own words, from a letter he wrote to me on 17 December 1977:

> I just received the score of the trombone piece, and it certainly brought back memories.
> John Cage came to my house in mid-town Manhattan one afternoon after having called me to ask if I were able to play the sliding trombone without having the notes written out in front of me. I more or less assumed that he was referring to the articulation of a jazz solo with a chordal reference and assured him that that was part of the business I was in and asked for a few more details. I had never heard of him at this time. About 10 minutes later, my doorbell rang and I met John for the first time.
> We spent much of the afternoon discussing many aspects of music, with my being critical of some of his theories and enthusiastic of others. I have long since learned that I had spent that afternoon wisely.
> I remember that we spent a long time with the instrument, taking it apart, playing without slide, without mouthpiece, adding various mutes, glass on the slide section, minus tuning slide, with spit valve open, and any other possibilities of producing a sound by either inhaling or exhaling air through a piece of metal tubing. We also discussed double stops, circular breathing, playing without moving slides, and on and on.
> I recall having mixed feelings as to whether I was working with a genius or someone of a slightly different bent.
> From these ideas we gathered together, we put forth a part that would be playable as a solo or in conjunction with a group of other players.
> I recall noting that the instructions said, "any part of these pages may be played, including none." That appealed to my sense of humor, and John and I became friends quickly.
> The piece was performed at New York Town Hall with (as I recall) a band of about 13 people, including some of the best classical and avant players in town. We had a standing room only audience with long lines of people being turned away.
> I believe it was recorded that night by George Avakian (I don't recall the company).[3] The performance that evening was good, but I personally felt that some of the players were having trouble realizing some of John's concepts about sound. We did 2 more performances later in the months to come and the players' response was absolutely thrilling. The idea of breaking with the traditional drill and beginning to make some hitherto unheard of sounds on the instruments was very appealing to me. I remember running up to John after the 3rd performance and lamenting the fact that we had not recorded it, since it was so much better than the first.
> During this period of years (I think the concert was 25 years of John Cage in retrospect — May 15th, 1958, Town Hall, New York), I did several other pieces with John, one of them being Theater Piece.
> John Cage has remained a very large influence in my thinking throughout my life . . . not only musically . . . but because many of his concepts directly overlap into everyday life processes. . . .

---

2. May 5, 1977, pp. 36-37.

3. *25 Year Retrospective Concert*, Avakian JCS-1.

Appendix V:
Range

There is much confusion regarding just what a composer should consider as the trombone range. This not only has to do with the equipment used but also the player. I am not much help, really, having been on the tenor trombone/bass trombone seesaw for a good part of my life.

HIGH RANGE

The extreme range of the trombone, for instance, in most orchestration books is said to go from, say, pedal G to the F above the tenor clef staff (see Example 1):

Example 1: Orchestration Book Extreme Range

However, many bass trombonists will say that the G or Ab below the high F should be the limit, realizing that the Bb or C above that is more typical as an extreme (see Example 2):

Example 2: Extreme High Range for Bass Trombone

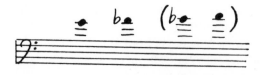

My bass trombone teacher, the late John Klock, insisted that the first thing to do in learning bass trombone is to thoroughly master the tenor trombone, and many concur with this (including myself). Of course, this includes the high F. Tenor trombone technique, at least at one time, included learning the "privileged" (or "falset") notes that I have come to know as "fake trigger" notes between the pedals and the low E just below the staff. One should consult Robin Gregory's *The Trombone*[1] for a full dis-

---

1. New York: Praeger, 1973.

cussion of this. In any case, in learning the bass trombone, much of the tenor technique (including these "fake trigger" notes) remains while the performer is acquiring the added elements.

PEDAL TONES

Pedal tones only partially solved the problem, for instance, of the various parts in such works as the Berg *Three Orchestra Pieces*, Op. 6 (1929).[2] In bar 155 of the third piece ("March"), all trombonists are, supposedly, to play notes marked "Pedalton," and, indeed, the fourth player *is* playing a pedal D (see Example 3):

Example 3: Berg *Three Orchestra Pieces*, Op. 6, Third Movement, Bars 154 and 155, Pedaltones in All Four Trombone Parts

The first trombonist, if using an alto trombone, will also play a real pedal tone an octave higher than the fourth part's pedal tone. The other two, and sometimes the first player as well, must use what in America is known as a large bore tenor with an "F" attachment or what in Europe is known as a "tenor-bass" trombone, since the second and third parts go quite high as well, up to the C# above the tenor clef staff. Of course, it may have been expected that the second and third parts would be played on tenor trombones using "fake trigger" notes, but this seems hardly likely. More than just a few composers may think of pedal tones as being *any* loud low note, since this sort of contradictory pedal indication is found more than just occasionally; the second and third parts are simply *not* pedal tones.[3]

---

2. Vienna: Universal Edition, 1954.

3. See Gregory, *The Trombone*, p. 62.

BARTÓK GLISSANDO

One interesting low-range problem is the famous third trombone glissando from the low B above the pedal Bb to the low F above, which appears in the Bartók *Concerto for Orchestra*[4] in the fourth movement in bar 90 (see Example 4):

Example 4: Bartók *Concerto for Orchestra*, Fourth Movement, Bar 90, Third Trombone Gliss

This is probably the most discussed problem glissando ever written, and the only instrument that this glissando seems to work on is the double Bb ("BBb" or "contrabass") trombone (with a double slide). However, the part is designed generally for bass trombone, not contrabass trombone.[5] My teacher, John Klock, bass trombonist with the San Francisco Symphony under Pierre Monteux for twenty-five years, stated (from his conversations with Monteux) that the Maestro had said, "Indeed, the old gentleman [Bartók] must have made a mistake." Whether he made a mistake or not may never be known, but it is safe to say that this one passage has been the single most influential factor in encouraging the development of the "double trigger" (two attachment valves) trombone. This does not really solve anything, for the break in the glissando still has to be covered, even with the aid of two valves.[6]

DOUBLE TRIGGER

Before the advent of the double trigger, many kinds of games were played with the Bartók glissando, probably the most common being the tuba taking the low B with the trombone picking up a lipped (bent toned) C that was a little flat and then finishing the gliss. This is only barely satisfactory, however, and the fact that the "double trigger" instrument is now becoming very common among bass trombonists is something to be welcomed with open arms. While still in a state of development and just now reaching a state of high quality (particularly in the handcrafted designs), its development is being hastened because of all the other advantages that have been discovered since its initial development.

There are two main advantages of the double trigger now. First, there is the inclusion of the low B natural into the mainstream of the "trigger-pedal" range, this range encompassing the pedal notes and the "missing" notes that the valve can obtain just below the bass clef staff (see Example 5):

---

4. London: Boosey and Hawkes, 1946.

5. George Maxted, in *Talking About the Trombone* (London: John Baker Ltd., 1970), pp. 34-35, provides a discussion of this glissando. His thought is that "the only real answer to this passage of course is the F trombone, for which I assume it must have been written, as this is the only instrument on which it would be possible to play the passage. This instrument is very cumbersome and is no longer in general use." It would be well to read his entire chapter (6) on "The Relationship of the Slide to Pitch," pp. 32-35.

6. Ibid., p. 34.

Example 5: Trigger-Pedal Range

The second main advantage is the general increase in technical facility in this same range. George Roberts, of Los Angeles, is the most famous and perhaps the first trombonist to popularize this facility among jazz bass trombonists and jazz arrangers. It has become the norm among bass trombonists ever since to really try to "get around" in that register, and, indeed, many have acquired a very good technical proficiency comparable to the other more normal registers.

This proficiency on the part of performers is affecting composers and how they write for bass trombone. It is bound to continue to help define the bass trombone as a separate entity; however, most composers will still not want to limit the top range in deference to bass trombone players, just as these same composers will often expect a comparable low range facility out of the tenor-bass trombone player.

TENOR-BASS

Because of composer demands and performer proficiency, the tenor-bass trombone is now a separate entity, although it really seems to have been born at about the same time as the Berg pieces mentioned earlier (the twenties). Stemming from this period, many works seem to call for the trombonist to go high *and* low a great deal. I have found, in my commissioning, that composers do not like to be limited with regard to range, and if there is any chance that a performer can (or will attempt) to go higher or lower, they will want this done. A notable exception in new music is the Berio *Sequenza V*, which is a real tenor trombone piece. This is due, no doubt, to the left hand's being continually occupied in front of the bell with the mute, and therefore unable to operate a trigger.

When asked the question about high range, I always state that the C# above the tenor clef staff is the last *really good* sounding high note. Above this the notes seem to pinch and tighten a bit, even in players who have them well developed. Some composers have taken this information seriously, such as Andrew Imbrie in his *Three Sketches*, going no higher than this C# but using that C# liberally. Others, such as Ernst Krenek in his *Five Pieces*, have the high F above the C#, or even a directive of "as high as possible," something which many composers do. These "as high as possible" directives can generally be assumed to be well above the high F. Incidentally, both the Krenek and the Imbrie works have considerable trigger activity.

ALTO TROMBONE

After a rather long eclipse in America, the alto trombone is once again gaining some favor in American orchestras. The resurrection of the *Concerto* by Albrechtsberger, in particular, has been helpful in reestablishing the instrument. During the period from 1962 to 1966, when I performed with the Oakland Symphony under Gerhard Samuel, I used an alto trombone for Mozart, Beethoven, and certain other composers' works, but I certainly felt that I was not conforming to the norm at all. However, through this period of eclipse in America, the alto maintained a moderate popularity in European orchestras. It has never had a dominant popularity, even in Europe, and I think this is due to the critical attention that must be paid to the alto trombone's intonation. Because the slide is shorter, the positions are close together; one does not have the same latitude of adjustment that one does on the tenor. The alto, however, has a unique and beautiful sound, and it is one which composers would find to their liking were the instrument more available. If one does choose to use the alto, one should keep in mind that most instruments are built in Eb; and while the alto will not necessarily *increase* the high range (as simple examination of the harmonic series would lead one to believe), it does bring to that existing high range a beautiful clarity not easily obtainable on the tenor trombone.

NEW LIMITS

The extremes of range can always be asked for, but there is a certain price to pay in using them, usually in some form of tone quality compromise. It is well, then, to study various works with regard to their range just to see how successfully or poorly this problem may have been handled. Despite what I have said about the *last good* high note, I also feel that there is no one single answer to fit all cases or even, for that matter, a few cases! The range question is interlinked inseparably with the piece as a whole and must be treated as such.

This question is interlinked with the player also. As jazz players are now setting new range limits, most symphonic players are becoming interested in obtaining these ranges as well. It has been discovered that the range can be extended down to pedal C and up to the octave above the high F mentioned before. Most bass trombonists, thanks to George Roberts, now consider playing the trigger-pedal range a normal thing to do, just as many players now play in the extra high octave with real technique in that extremity. It is not as easy to pin down just who was first in getting "way *up* there," but, in any case, Bill Watrous seemingly says it all with his Columbia recording.[7] Who is to say at this point that the peaks and valleys have all been reached?

---

7. *Bill Watrous Manhattan Wildlife Refuge*, Columbia Records KC 33090.

Bibliography

BOOKS AND ARTICLES

Baker, David. *Contemporary Techniques for the Trombone*. New York: Charles Colin, 1974.
___. *Jazz Styles and Analysis: Trombone*. Chicago: down beat Music Workshop Publications (db/MWP Cat. No. 8), Maher Publications, 1973.
Bridges, Glenn. *Pioneers in Brass*. Detroit: Sherwood Publications, 1965. (Available from the author, 15626 Callahan, Fraser, Michigan 48026.)
Carse, Adam. *Musical Wind Instruments*. New York: Da Capo Press, 1965.
Coar, Birchard. *A Critical Study of the 19th-Century Horn Virtuosi in France*. De Kalb, Illinois: B. Coar, 1952.
Elkin, A. P. *The Australian Aborigines*. 4th ed. Sydney: Angus and Robertson, 1964.
Ellington, Duke. *Music Is My Mistress*. New York: Doubleday, 1973.
Erickson, Robert. *Sound Structure in Music*. Los Angeles: University of California Press, 1975.
Everett, Thomas. *Annotated Guide to Bass Trombone Literature*. Nashville: The Brass Press, 1973.
Fink, Reginald. *The Trombonist's Handbook*. Athens, Ohio: Accura Music, 1970 and 1977.
Gregory, Robin. *The Trombone*. New York: Praeger, 1973.
Hoffnung, Gerard. *The Hoffnung Symphony Orchestra*. London: Dennis Dobson, 1955.
Jones, Trevor A. "The Didjeridu," in *Studies in Music*, Vol. 1. Perth: University of Western Australia Press, 1967.
Kennan, Kent. *Technique of Orchestration*. 2nd ed. New York: Prentice-Hall, 1970.
Kleinhammer, Edward. *The Art of Trombone Playing*. Evanston, Illinois: Summy-Birchard Co., 1963.
Lazarus, Arnold. "Amplification and Electronic Effects," Chapter 7 in Turetzky's *The Contemporary Contrabass* (see below under Turetzky).
MacArthur, Douglas. *Reminiscenes*. New York: McGraw-Hill, 1964.
Maxted, George. *Talking About the Trombone*. London: John Baker Ltd., 1970.
Nichols, Keith. "Muted Brass," in *Storyville* No. 30. London: Storyville, August-September, 1970.
Piston, Walter. *Orchestration*. New York: W. W. Norton, 1955.
Praetorius, Michael. *Syntagma Musicum*, Vol. II, Translated by Harold Blumenfeld, 2nd Ed. New York: Bärenreiter, 1962.
Rehak, Frank. "Interview," in *down beat*. Chicago: down beat publications, May 5, 1977.
Scholes, Percy A. *Oxford Companion to Music*, 10th Ed. London: Oxford University Press, 1970.
Sloan, Gerald. "The Talking Trombone in Jazz," in the *Journal of the International Trombone Association*, Vol. VI. Normal, Illinois: International Trombone Association, January, 1978.
Tomita, T. Peter. "Stu Dempster at and/or," in *Ear*, Vol. 4, No. 7. Berkeley: Ear, Fall, 1976.
Turetzky, Bertram. *The Contemporary Contrabass*. Los Angeles: University of California Press, 1974.
Wick, Dennis. *Trombone Technique*. London: Oxford University Press, 1973.
Wilding-White, Raymond. *Twentieth-Century Techniques*. New York: Holt, Rinehart, and Winston, to be released soon.
Wilson, Phil. "The Great Jazz Trombone Stylists," in *The Instrumentalist*, Evanston, Illinois: The Instrumentalist, February 1974.

MUSIC

Albrechtsberger, Johann Georg. *Concerto for Alto Trombone and Strings* (1769). Budapest: Editio Musica, 1968.
Alsina, Carlos Roqué. *Consecuenza for Trombone Solo* (1966). Berlin: Bote and Bock, 1969.
Austin, Larry. *CHANGES: Open Style for Trombone and Magnetic Tape* (1965). Sacramento, California: Composer Performer Edition, 1965.

Bark, Jan, and Folke Rabe. *Bolos for Four Trombones* (1962). Stockholm: Wilhelm Hansen, 1964.

Bartók, Béla. *Concerto for Orchestra*. London: Boosey and Hawkes, 1946.

Berg, Alban. *Three Pieces for Orchestra*, Op. 6. Vienna: Universal, 1954.

Bergsma, William. *Blatant Hypotheses for Trombone and Percussion* (1977). New York: Galaxy Music Corp., 1979.

Bernstein, Leonard. *Elegy for Mippy II for Solo Trombone*. New York: G. Schirmer, 1950.

Berio, Luciano. *Sequenza V for Trombone Solo* (1966). London: Universal Edition, 1968.

Bruce, Neely. *Grand Duo for Trombone and Piano* (1971), manuscript.

Cage, John. *Solo for Sliding Trombone* (1957-58). New York: Henmar Press, sole distributors C. F. Peters, 1960.

Childs, Barney. *First Brass Quintet* (1954), manuscript.

____. *Music for Trombone and Piano* (1966). New York: American Composers Alliance, 1966.

____. *Sonata for Solo Trombone* (1961). Bryn Mawr, Pennsylvania: Tritone Press, sole distributors Theodore Presser, 1962.

deJong, Conrad. *Aanraking (Contact) for Solo Trombone* (1969). New York: G. Schirmer, 1970.

De Leeuw, Ton. *Music for Trombone* (1973-74). Amsterdam: Donemus, 1974.

Druckman, Jacob. *Animus I for Trombone and Tape* (1966). New York: MCA Music, 1967.

du Bois, Rob. *Music for a Sliding Trombone* (1968). Amsterdam: Donemus, 1968.

Erb, Donald. *. . . and then, toward the end . . . for Trombone and Tape* (1971). Bryn Mawr, Pennsylvania: Theodore Presser, 1972.

____. *Concerto for Trombone and Orchestra* (1976). Bryn Mawr, Pennsylvania: Theodore Presser, 1976.

____. *In No Strange Land for Contrabass, Trombone, and Tape* (1968), manuscript.

Erickson, Robert. *General Speech for Solo Trombone* (1969). New York: Okra Music Corp., 1976.

____. *Ricercare á 5 for Trombones* (1966). New York: Okra Music Corp., 1971.

Fillmore, Henry. *Lassus Trombone*. New York: Fillmore, 1918.

Gershwin, George. *Rhapsody in Blue for Piano and Orchestra*. New York: Harms, 1942.

Globokar, Vinko. *Discours pour 5 trombones* (1967-68). New York: C. F. Peters, 1970.

Hughes, Robert. *Anagnorisis, a Ballet for Trombone, Percussion, and Solo Dancer* (1964), manuscript.

Imbrie, Andrew. *Three Sketches for Trombone and Piano* (1967). London: Malcolm Music, Ltd., 1970.

Johnston, Ben. *One Man for Trombonist and Percussion* (1967 and 1972). Urbana, Illinois: Media Press, 1975.

Krenek, Ernst. *Five Pieces for Trombone and Piano* (1967). Kassel, West Germany: Bärenreiter, 1969.

London, Edwin. *Hi-Lites (1973) from the Carnivore of Uranus for Trombone and Tape* (1972), manuscript.

Moran, Robert. *Bombardments No. 4 for Trombone and Tape* (1964 and 1968), manuscript.

Mueller, Robert. *Schule Fuer Zugposaune*. Frankfurt: Wilhelm Zimmerman, 1902.

____. *Technical Studies for Trombone*. New York: Carl Fischer, 1924.

Mumma, Gordon. *Hornpipe for Cybersonic French Horn* (1967), manuscript.

Oliveros, Pauline. *Theater Piece for Trombone Player and Tape* (1966), manuscript.

Rabe, Folke, and Jan Bark. (See under Bark.)

Reynolds, Roger. *". . . From Behind the Unreasoning Mask" for Trombone, Percussion, and Tape* (1974). New York: C. F. Peters, 1975.

Schwartz, Elliott. *Options for Trombone Soloist and Grand Piano* (with additional options for accompaniment by percussionist, electronic tape, or percussionist and tape — 1970), manuscript.

____. *Signals for Trombone and Contrabass* (1968), manuscript.

Stravinsky, Igor. *Pulcinella*. London: Boosey and Hawkes, 1966.

Suderburg, Robert. *Chamber Music III, Night Set for Trombone and Piano* (1971). Bryn Mawr, Pennsylvania: Theodore Presser, 1979.

Weber, C. M. von. *Horn Concertino*, Op. 45. Wiesbaden: Breitkopf and Härtel, 1960.

Wilding-White, Raymond. *Encores for Stu* (for trombone and various combinations — 1970), manuscript.

____. *Whatzit No. 6 for Trombone and Tape* (1970), manuscript.

RECORDINGS
Listed alphabetically by trombonist (other pertinent recordings follow)

Anderson, Miles, trombone. *Miles Anderson Plays His Slide Trombone*. Avant 1006 (includes Barney Childs's *Sonata for Solo Trombone* and Harold Budd's *only three clouds*).

____. *The Music of Roger Reynolds (and others)*. New World Records NW 237 (includes Roger Reynolds's *". . . From Behind the Unreasoning Mask" for Trombone, Percussion, and Tape*).

Betters, Harold. *Out of Sight and Sound*. Reprise No. 6208.

Dempster, Stuart, trombone. *Acoustic Research Contemporary Music Project No. 2* (in conjunction with Deutsche Grammophon), AR 2 — 0654 084 (includes Robert Erickson's *Ricercare á 5 for Trombones*).

___. *Music for Instruments and Electronic Sounds.* Nonesuch H 71223 (includes Donald Erb's *In No Strange Land for Trombone, Bass, and Tape*).

___. *New Music for Virtuosos No. 2.* New World Records, NW 254 (includes Robert Erickson's *General Speech for Solo Trombone* and Andrew Imbrie's *Three Sketches for Trombone and Piano*).

___. *Stuart Dempster in the Great Abbey of Clement VI.* 1750 Arch Records S-1775 (includes Stuart Dempster's *Standing Waves — 1976* and *Didjeridervish — 1976*).

Globokar, Vinko, trombone. *Vinko Globokar, Trombone.* DGG avant garde 137-005 (includes Carlos Roqué Alsina's *Consecuenza for Trombone Solo,* Luciano Berio's *Sequenza V for Trombone Solo,* Vinko Globokar's *Discourse II for Five Trombones,* and Karlheinz Stockhausen's *Solo for Melody Instrument and Tape*).

Griffin, Dick, trombone. *The Eighth Wonder Dick Griffin.* Strata-East SES-19747.

Lashley, Lester, trombone. *Sound, Roscoe Mitchell Sextet.* Delmark DS-9408.

Lewis, George, trombone. *The George Lewis Solo Trombone Record.* Sackville 3012.

Mangelsdorff, Albert, trombone. *Trombirds.* BASF — MPS 21-21654-3

Rudd, Roswell, trombone. *Archie Shepp Live in San Francisco.* Impulse A-9118 (includes *Wherever June Bugs Go*).

___. *Everywhere — Roswell Rudd.* Impulse A-9126.

Rutherford, Paul, trombone. *The Gentle Harm of the Bourgeoisie.* Emanem 3305.

Smith, Andre, trombone. *Electronic Music III.* Turnabout Vox TV 34177 (includes Jacob Druckman's *Animus I for Trombone and Tape*).

Thelin, Eje, trombone. *Eje Thelin Group.* Caprice RIKS LP 91.

Watrous, Bill. *Bill Watrous Manhattan Wildlife Refuge.* Columbia Records KC 33090.

Wells, Dickie (All Stars). *Bone Four-in-Hand.* MJR 8118.

Wilson, Phil, trombone. *The Sound of the Wasp — Phil Wilson and Rich Matteson.* ASI Records ASI-203.

– –

Cage, John. *25 Year Retrospective Concert.* Avakian JCS-1.

Horn, Paul. *Inside the Great Pyramid.* Mushroom Records MRS 5507.

___. *Inside the Taj Mahal.* Epic Stereo BXN 26466.

Jones, Spike. *The Best of Spike Jones.* RCA Victor LSP-3849(e).

___. *Spike Jones is Murdering the Classics.* RCA Red Seal LSC-3235(e).

Moyle, Alice. *Songs from the Northern Territory.* Available from the Australian Institute of Aboriginal Studies, P.O. Box 553, Canberra City, A. C. T. 2601, or Humanities Press Inc., 171 First Avenue, Atlantic Highlands, New Jersey 07716.

___. *Aboriginal Sound Instruments.* Soon to be released — will be available from the same addresses noted immediately above.

Mumma, Gordon (and others). *Sonic Arts Union — Electric Sound.* Mainstream Records MS/5010 (includes Mumma's *Hornpipe for Cybersonic French Horn*).

The Music of Tibet — The Tantric Rituals. Anthology Records AST-4005. Available from Anthology Record and Tape Corp., 135 W. 41st St., New York, New York 10036.

Index

Compositor: University of California Press
Printer: Malloy Lithographing, Inc.
Binder: Riverside Book Bindery
Text: CompSet 500 Times Roman
Display: CompSet 500 Baskerville
Paper: 60 lb. Williamsburg Wove